DELIVER ME FROM MY ANGUISH, LORD!

BIBLICAL PRINCIPLES TO OVERCOME DEPRESSION

by RUTHIE VELAZQUEZ-PAREDES

Copyright © 2012 by RUTHIE VELAZQUEZ-PAREDES

DELIVER ME FROM MY ANGUISH, LORD!
by RUTHIE VELAZQUEZ-PAREDES

Printed in the United States of America

ISBN 9781622305056

All rights reserved solely by the author. The author guarantees all contents are original and do not infringe upon the legal rights of any other person or work. No part of this book may be reproduced in any form without the permission of the author. The views expressed in this book are not necessarily those of the publisher.

Unless otherwise indicated, Bible quotations are taken from the King James Version of the Bible.

www.xulonpress.com

Table of Content

Dedication	ix
Note of Recognition	xi
Foreword	xiii
Introduction	xv
God Always Has a Purpose	19
What is Anguish?	28
Looking at Anguish With a Spiritual Lens	33
Opening the Doors of my Heart	39
The Spirit of Anguish Has Always Existed	44
Anguish As a Result of our Trials	50
It All Starts In Your Mind	54
We Are Members of One Body	63
It Is Not a Sin to Feel Momentary Anguish	66
What Happens When I Let the Spirit of Anguish Control me?	78
It's Time to Change	89
How Can I Be Free?	92
God Has Everything under Control	105
Where Do I Start?	119
The Spirit of Anguish Will Mold Our Character	130
God Loved Us First	141
Bibliography	143

DELIVER ME FROM MY ANGUISH, LORD!

Dedication and Acknowledgements

First and foremost, I would like to dedicate this book to my beloved Lord and Savior, to whom I live grateful for his abundant blessings and for giving me the opportunity to carry His message through his Word into the lives of those crying out: Deliver me from my anguish, Lord!

I want to thank in a very special way my beloved husband, Juan Carlos Paredes, who has been the driving force behind this project and also the special editor. Thank you for your love, your support, your invaluable help, and for making me so happy.

I also dedicate this work to the memory of my holy mother, Ana Elsie Hernández—a unique woman of God and prayer warrior who went to dwell with the Lord in June 2008.

I am grateful to Iglesia Cristiana Puertas Abiertas (Open Doors Christian Church) and to my pastor and my brother, Ray David Velázquez, in Tampa, Florida, for their support and collaboration to make this project a reality. My three children: David, Jonathan and Joshua. May this book be an inspiration for their lives and may it motivate them to find true happiness found only in Christ Jesus, the one and only Savior—to whom glory belongs now and forever. Amen.

Note of Recognition

Executive Producer: Juan Carlos Paredes

Editor: Daphne Tarango

Graphics: www.idsdesigns.com

Photographer: Ismari Lopez

Professional collaboration: Rosita Sierra

Originally Published in Spanish as:

¡Libértame de la Angustia, Señor!

Foreword

Dear reader, before reading this book, I would like for you to ask yourself these questions:

- Do I cry often without knowing why?
- Do I find myself visiting moments of the past again and again in my mind?
- Do I spend time reviewing things from the past and wondering what could I have done to make things better?
- Do I often think that God has forgotten me?
- Do I feel depressed?
- Have I lost the desire to worship God and to thank Him for all his blessings?
- Do I frequently recall my past sins?
- Do I worry about things that have no remedy or about things that have not yet happened?
- Am I routinely looking for an excuse for not attending any invitation to a social event or family gatherings?
- Am I routinely looking for a reason not to fellowship with others?

If you answered yes to any of these questions or you know someone who may be in this situation, then it is possible that you or someone you know is being tormented by the spirit of anguish. To you, I dedicate this book in particular, with all humility and with love. I hope it will be a great blessing to your life and that through the Word of God you may be totally free of the spirit of anguish.

Many people are faced with anguish when they go through a life event. In this book, we will be brief review of the entire Bible, discovering the characters who remain great men and women of God but who also experienced moments of anguish. God glorified himself in each one of them by enabling them to make it to the other side. You must put much effort in wanting to be free from the spirit of anguish. Allow God to work within you and help you be the person He wants you to be and to face life with courage and dignity.

INTRODUCTION

At the end of the 1990s, as we approached a new century, panic and uncertainty overwhelmed many people in all parts of the world. It was thought that technology and science were not prepared to cope with the changes that would come. There was so much anguish that people were affected as a result of all the speculations. Many people thought it would be the end of the world. Many were filled with unrest and some committed foolish acts. Wise men, intellectuals, and even scientists thought something big would happen when the clock marked the end of the twentieth century and we entered into the new century. Some men sought to create shelters in the event of a catastrophe. Everyone was expecting the worst. Concern and uncertainty toward this panic grew as a suspense movie as we grew closer to this date. When the bells chimed on December 31, 1999, the year 2000 was here!

The world seemed to stop at a fraction a second and all were baffled when they realized that everything was continuing as normal and nothing drastic happened as speculated by many. Computers were not affected as was thought, nor did a global disaster take place as expected by many. The world did not cease to exist, and Earth did not disappear from the universe—as many had projected. How much concern, how much anguish of possible pain and tragedy—all in vain because that something did not take place!

What man does not want to understand is that God has all the control, not only of what can be happening in the life of an individual, as well as every detail that occurs on the face of the earth. Nothing can intimidate the children of God. The Christian who truly has had a personal experience with God knows he or she is planted on the rock of ages that is Jesus Christ. We remain even stronger when the strong wind of life and the storms chastise us severely and without compassion, for the Lord our God is with us.

Did you know that every moment you spend feeling distressed is time missing out from being happy and enjoying life? God wants you to be happy. There are times in our lives when we have to face the unexpected. There are times in our lives when things suddenly change and we have to make decisions, not because we want to but because circumstances demand it. That is why we must try, as much as possible, to keep our minds free from concerns that can cause distress and further bring anguish to our life. With a clear mind, we focus on the reality of what happens to us, as well as make decisions that are favorable for us, the people we love, and all those who are around us. A person tormented by anguish is not capable of making smart decisions of any kind because he or she does not have a clear mind and cannot see beyond the suffering they are enduring at the time. We should not be surprised when we feel haunted by things

INTRODUCTION

that may happen to us. After all, we are in this world and we are made of flesh and bone. It is when we allow such suffering to take control of our feelings and we lose focus to such a degree that it does not allow us to see the complete picture of what God is doing backstage in the midst of our storm. There is great danger when our actions and decisions are the result of anguish.

As Christians, you and I cannot judge things like the world judges things. Nor should we mourn in times of sorrow to the brink of madness—although in our humanity, that is precisely what our mind tells us to do. What matters is that when we realize our anguish, we not let ourselves fall into this mindset and allow it to control our feelings. If we allow anguish to create an abyss between reality and our feelings, we will not be able to make it to the other side on our own.

The Apostle Paul, writing to the believers in Thessalonica, urged them to always be joyful. The joy of the Lord gives us the strength to stand up and to move forward. Nehemiah 8:10 says the joy of the Lord is our strength. There is a huge difference between the joy that the world offers and the joy that Jesus offers. I do not expect that the unsaved will understand this concept of always being joyful—even when we experience anguish.

Job 20:5 says the joy of the wicked is for a moment. Romans 12:12 tells us to be joyful in hope, patient in tribulation. And the verse that crowns my thinking to explain this type of joy is 2 Corinthians 6:10: "As sorrowful, yet always rejoicing; as poor, yet making many rich; as having nothing, and yet possessing all things."

During the past few years, I have encountered many people who are being tormented by a spirit of anguish that won't let them live at peace. It is something I myself have experienced. I have been visited by this horrible feeling, which is why I believe that God has placed on my shoulders a burden to share what I have been able to understand by the word of God about this topic.

Today, this world is in economic, social, and mental turmoil. A desire has been birthed within me to bring to light truths about this topic. I have spent a great deal of time studying and meditating on the things God has shown me and on the things I have experienced in my own life. From the moment I started to dig deeper into this topic, I asked God for wisdom and discernment. I asked Him to expose my own feelings on the topic so I may encourage and bless all who read these words. I must admit that I have had many personal and spiritual struggles since I started to work on this project. When I committed myself to the task of understanding the significance of this word with the goal of ministering to others directly from the Word of God, I learned that this issue is very too deep and complex to explain briefly, but I will do my best.

There are many aspects of this topic that I may not be able to explain in depth in one volume. However, with the leading and the inspiration of the Holy Spirit, we will be able to instill hope in someone who privately cries out, "Deliver me from my anguish, Lord." If this happens, we will have achieved our goal. To God be the glory!

God always has a purpose

A few years ago, while living in North Carolina, I became acquainted with a woman of God with whom I became friends. This friend has a doctorate in Biblical Theology. When I met her, I felt as if we had known each other our whole lives. Over a cup of coffee, I opened my heart and told the story of my life and the many things that were causing me anguish and had led to my spiritual ruin. I felt within me a great need to express to her all the things I had experienced, giving detailed explanations of many things from my past. While I opened my heart, I could not avoid a feeling of anguish. I cried because of my spiritual condition at that time. It was as if a finger pointed directly at me in an accusatory way, telling me, "How could you have been so ungrateful and failed the Lord? How could you?" I heard so many questions in my mind.

My friend watched and listened very quietly as I spoke. When I finished, she spoke a word into my life. God revealed many things to her at that precise moment. Although I do not remember in detail everything she said to me that evening, one thing was engraved on my mind and heart. She told me I was going through a process of internal healing and that was the reason God wanted to take me to

North Carolina: To deal with me away from my comfort zone—Florida. She went on to say that there would come a day when God would glorify Himself in my life in a very special way. I would be a vessel in His hands again.

Although I didn't understand the reasons behind some of her words to me that night, God revealed to her that my story would help other people who are going through the same situation I had experienced and that my testimony would help them to understand not only that God has a purpose for their lives but also to help them get back up in the name of the Lord. I had no idea how all this was going to be possible because the furthest thing from my mind was that God would restore me to the ministry. More specifically, I was almost convinced that God no longer loved me and that He had dismissed me as His minister for having failed Him. I felt unworthy to pronounce his Word on my lips. The thought alone caused me great distress. Little did I understand what the Apostle Paul wrote in his epistle in Romans 11:29, "For God's gifts and His call are irrevocable."

The sad reality is that people are very quick to judge and to cast you aside forever. Many people kick others when they are down. However, God in His infinite mercy rises from the mud whom He wants, when He wants, how He wants. This we know from Philippians 2:13: "For it is God who works in you both to will and to act according to His good purpose."

In May 2003, precisely the same day I was to move back to Florida, I was visited by the spirit of anguish. I had all my furniture and belongings ready in storage. I wanted to finish my last day at work before leaving North Carolina. I was staying with a friend and had mailed a ticket for someone to come up to North Carolina to accompany me on my drive down to Florida. The day finally arrived. Early in the morning, the person called to tell me he had missed his flight from Florida to North Carolina. At that moment, I felt I did not have many options, as I had already resigned and was anxious to arrive in Florida as soon as possible, search for a job, and get settled.

I could not believe my ears, and I got very angry. After ending the phone call, I started to pace from one side of my apartment to the other, complaining and asking God, "How can this be possible?" I stood in front of the mirror complaining and wondering why these things kept happening to me. I started to play a CD by a Christian singer who had gone to be with the Lord, Vanessa López. I started to prepare myself for my last day at work, so I could see my colleagues as they bid me farewell. The anguish and anger that seized me at that moment was so strong that I gritted my teeth and could not contain the tears that streamed from my eyes and down my cheeks. The music was still playing when I heard the following lyrics: "I went down on my knees and I cried 'Holy, holy, holy, to the lamb of God.'" Suddenly, I felt the Holy Spirit begin to speak through my own mouth in another language that was neither Spanish nor English. They were beautiful tongues, but I could understand as He spoke to my heart, telling me He had everything under control. He went on to say that whatever I didn't understand at that time, I would understand later. I sensed that God was with me, and I fell on my knees. I began to ask the Lord's forgiveness for not having trusted in Him. I was more concerned about the eleven-hour journey that I didn't realize that God had allowed this for a reason. I realized that my anguish and anger weren't allowing me to focus on preparing "plan B."

After having remained on my knees and in silence for a while listening to the voice of God speaking to my heart, I got up and washed my face with a new attitude. I already knew the route and could drive to Florida without any problems, so I decided to head out with confidence. After saying goodbye to my friend at the apartment where I had been staying, I drove to work, where my colleagues waited to say goodbye. I had swollen eyes from crying. When I arrived, they had prepared a surprise farewell party. This also made me cry, but this time, they were tears of joy. They gave me gifts, cards, and flowers— a huge surprise and special treat because I had only been working there nine months. I felt God's grace surrounding me.

It was around three o'clock in the afternoon when I finally said goodbye to my colleagues. At that time, the company for which I worked in Greensboro, North Carolina, was facing a financial situation, and their future was unstable. After a while, I learned that their fate was in the hands of a few lawyers. They would decide whether the company would close its operations or sell the division to another company, thus helping employees to keep their jobs. As I left the building—on my way down the stairs, I found myself crying again, asking God to take charge of that situation to avoid the possibility that my coworkers would lose their jobs. Months later, I learned that there was no need to close the operations, but that all were able to keep their jobs. I am sure that it was God who worked behind the scenes.

I took Interstate 40 and headed to Florida—my car loaded with the few belongings I had. My eyes were very tired of crying—it had been a day of many emotions and feelings and I felt as if I could fall asleep. But I felt the power of God on my life in a supernatural way, so I did not let myself be carried away by what I was feeling. My spirit was joyful.

I had only been on the road about 25 minutes when I felt as if a hand grabbed my right foot and placed it on the brake pedal, bringing my car to a full stop in the middle of the interstate. A cloud covered the windshield, and I couldn't see anything. I had not realized that a swirl of sand had formed on the road and prevented visibility. I was astonished when I realized that my car was in front of an aluminum standing in front an aluminum exit separator which detours from the interstate in a road to where I was going directly to crash myself in my car. Without a doubt, if God had not intervened by stopping my car on time, the accident would have been fatal. Instantly, I rested my forehead on the steering wheel and gave thanks to God, and there I learned that the one who would lead the automobile during the entire trip was God himself—not me.

During the eleven long hours of driving home, I listened to Christian music. Some moments I would turn everything off and allow God to speak to my mind and my heart. I could feel His presence in a supernatural way. I could feel him by my side. I will never forget that journey, and although I could never express how God dealt with my life during that time, I did understand that once again, God delivered me from the spirit of anguish, that I could not hinder His plans for me, and that I could move forward.

On September 11 of the year 2001, our nation suffered the biggest hit of its history, when the twin towers in New York were knocked down. They were times of great anguish and despair, not only for those who were directly affected by the loss of a loved one, but for the whole world. For many of the relatives and friends of those who perished that day, their lives would never be the same again. It was the day before my birthday, and I can assure you that there was no celebrating for me the next day. There are still many people who are feeling the effects of the ravages of this unprecedented event.

Currently, the world faces an economic crisis. Experts in the field have declared a global recession. Everywhere we hear many say that they are concerned because they fear losing their jobs or their homes. Thousands of people are struggling with debt. Others are worried about how to move forward as they're confronted with price increases but constant wages. Many cannot even sleep at night; some get sick to their stomachs, with headaches and panic attacks. Others have thought that suicide was the only way out and have ended their lives. They did not receive the gift of peace that Christ offers. Christ said: "My peace I leave with you; my peace I give unto

God always has a purpose

you, not as the world gives, I give to you." Inner peace and peace of mind is the peace that Christ brings. Later Christ said: "Let not your heart be troubled, neither let it be afraid" (John 14:27). The peace which is referred to here is that which is mentioned in Philippians 4:7, "And the peace of God, which surpasses all understanding, shall keep your hearts and minds through Christ Jesus." In other words, it is a calm attitude that envelopes —one no one can understand—even in the midst of the storms of life.

Some years ago, I met a woman named Maria. We called her Mary. She was a very happy, ready at work and very attentive with all those who came in contact with her. Her smile was beautiful and contagious, and in a short time we formed a nice friendship. On some occasions, we would go to her home at lunch time. One day, she showed me a huge basket—a flower arrangement full of dry roses that her husband had given her over the years.

My friend routinely talked to me about the happiness she shared with her husband and her children. They were her world. I came to admire her in great way, simply for the beautiful person she was. I always pictured them as having the ideal marriage. They had already been married more than twenty years, but they loved each other so much more than the first day of their marriage. When I moved to North Carolina, I lost contact with her.

On a particular evening upon returning to Florida, I was at a cell group at the home of a church member. One man's face was very familiar to me, but I could not place it. After some conversation, I realized he was Juan, Mary's husband. I was ecstatic! I would finally hear how my friend was doing. Very excited, I asked right away about Mary, his wife. I remember Juan bowing his head and gazing at the floor. A few seconds of silence passed, and with a knot in his throat, he told me she had died—a victim of cancer just two years before. You can imagine how sad I felt! Tears welled up in my eyes as I listened to Juan describe his sad and poignant story of the loss of his beloved Mary. This was the last thing I ever expected to hear. As you can imagine, the loss of his Mary was a very hard blow for him.

I did not yet understand how he had come to know the Lord, so I wanted him to tell me how he had met Jesus and was now serving God and attending a Christian church. He told me that losing his wife was very painful for him. He cried without consolation day and night. He could not work, eat, or sleep, and his life was meaningless.

Daily, without exception, this man would visit his wife's tomb at the cemetery; there he spent long hours lying on the grave. Many times, he would fall asleep in the cemetery until afternoon. A spirit of anguish had taken over him—much stronger than his own will. One morning, he got up to go to the cemetery as was his custom. That day, he decided to stay there until he died. For the first time en route to the cemetery, he realized there was a Christian church on the same road. As he approached the church, he felt a strong urging to go inside. He heard a voice that bid him to come in. He decided to obey, parked his car, and entered the sanctuary. There he met several pastors. They welcomed him and asked if they could help him. Upon telling them his story, they prayed for him, and God delivered him of the spirit of anguish, filling him with joy and happiness. After praying on his knees for a while, he arose with new strength and hope. Surely he still felt sadness in the human sense, but now he felt the peace of God which surpassed all understanding in his heart.

When Christ enters man's heart, He fills him with indescribable peace and all things change. Therein lies the great difference: The problems are still there, but God helps him to cope with the burden. With time, this man was able to overcome his great loss, allowing the Lord to heal his pain and continue his life. He realized that by dwelling close to God, it was easier to deal with life. He began to see things from God's perspective and had the strength to get back up.

As Christians, we have experienced the love of God, by which we can understand and accept that behind everything that happens in our life, God always has a purpose.

What is anguish?

According to the dictionary, the words anguish, tribulation and grief can all be synonymous. They define these words as "a cry for help," "a bitter suffering or grief," or terrible pain of the body and mind. Grief and drug addiction can all be related to emotional distress or feeling "miserable and discouraged." You can also describe this as: adversity, misery, suffering, destruction, suffering and tribulation. All of these things produce great burden in a person's spirit, snatching peace even from the children of God.

When we asked the Mental Health Family Counselor, Rosita Sierra, about her thoughts on the subject of anguish, her remarks were as follows: "Everyone has a certain level of stress in their lives, which can cause distress. Some things seem to be so distressing that they can take over our mind. It is easier for some people to manage the pain and disappointment than it is for others. It all depends on the ability of a person to adapt to the situation and person's state of mind when confronted with anguish." Rosita Sierra explains: "If the person is not able to adapt, they run the risk of developing a psychological disorder, which could have a direct effect on their ability to function in their daily environment, including home and family life and even in their workplace."

"Because there is a strong connection between the mind and the rest of the body, a person's health can also be affected as a result of anguish." In addition, a person who is in anguish is not fully aware of his or her surroundings. They can also feel worthless and hopeless, which could lead the person to consider suicide. It is also possible that the person's anxiety may lead him or her to abuse or addiction — including drugs, alcohol, illegal behavior, and even promiscuity. The person is likely looking for a way to alleviate pain or to fill a void with something that makes them feel good — even temporarily. People who have gone through some trauma are at highest risk of feeling anguish and its consequences. Trauma may arise because of abuse, domestic violence, sexual violence, accidents, war, and natural disasters, among others. If the person does not face the situation in a direct way, they are prone to develop post-traumatic stress disorder, anxiety, depression, or other mental disorders. Their lives can be affected forever if the situation is not dealt with in a timely manner.

How to get out of Anguish?

As not all react to anguish in the same way, what works for one person may not work for another. The best thing is to find what works best for that particular person.

First of all, the person must want to change. If the person persists in thinking about what causes them distress, the person will remain stagnant. This individual must voluntarily be willing to experience a change in his life. Some people have a greater tolerance in the midst of anguish and are willing to try different methods to improve the situation. Others prefer to take medications prescribed by a doctor or psychiatrist. Medications can help to improve the person's daily functioning, but they also may bandage the wound, covering it temporarily without providing a direct cure. Many choose to speak with a family member, someone they trust, or a professional such as a therapist or a spiritual advisor. In many cases, it is recommended that the person have a support system to help them deal with the anguish. Those who have some sort of support can usually deal with the situation much better than those who do not. It is also beneficial for the person to cope with their distress with their spiritual beliefs, learning to rely on the power of God—not on his own strength. Prayer and meditation can help a person to focus on a Higher Power and feel confident that they are not fighting alone. By leaning on their spiritual beliefs, the person often discovers his real purpose in life and learns to accept and understand the reasons for the events in their life. Having a sense of purpose in life fills them with the necessary hope and faith to face their anguish.

It is important that the person identify their strengths and the good things they have to offer. In many cases, the person is so focused on the negative aspects of his life that they become accustomed to the negative. If a person can control his thoughts and keep a positive outlook, the likelihood increases that they will overcome their anguish. Identifying the good qualities in a person will help them to begin feeling better about themselves. When we experience anguish, we worry about the possibility that something terrible might happen over which we have no control and we would feel useless to cope. We can also define anguish as an unexpected—and often, unknown—threat that makes us appear incompetent and ridiculous at any given time. Distress can be caused by things that happen unexpectedly and affect our emotions permanently.

Anguish can become a vicious cycle. I have noted that when a person experiences anguish for no apparent reason, they become distressed at the thought of future situations. Thoughts such as "it would be awful if I started to feel distressed" will surface. Thinking this way provokes anxiety, which not only increases the anguish but also leads the person to think, "I am losing control" or "What if I faint or have a panic attack? What if I'm crazy? What if I'm getting a heart attack?" Anguish multiplies and leads to further distressing thoughts and panicky feelings. The primary sign of anxiety is that, little by little, the person generalizes the feelings and over time, more things produce their anxiety.

According to the Manual for Diagnosis of Mental Disorders, a panic attack is a timed and isolated fear or severe condition that is accompanied by four (or more) of the following symptoms, beginning abruptly and reaching its maximum in the first ten minutes:

- Heart palpitations or elevated heart rate
- Sweating
- Tremors or shaking

- Suffocation or shortness of breath
- Choking
- Oppression or chest discomfort
- Nausea or abdominal discomfort
- Instability, dizziness, or fainting
- Daydreaming or disassociation
- Fear of losing control or going crazy
- Fear of dying
- Paresthesia (numbness or tingling)
- Chills or hot flashes

Anguish is psychological venom that can cause much damage; however, with the help of a professional, it is possible to learn not only to control the symptoms and its consequences on the body but also to eliminate the sources of fear and stress. Participating in behavior management may offer good results.

Looking at Anguish with a Spiritual Lens

I do not intend to diminish the value or importance of the information I've presented above; however, I want to focus on anguish from a spiritual point of view. The contents of this book are the expression of a born-again person. I am someone who lives very thankful to God for having been delivered from grief repeatedly. Throughout this book, I'm willing to share my experiences to help others understand that God is our deliverer. It is my sincere desire to give by grace what, by grace, has been given to me. I open my heart and offer my treasures and personal experiences so that God would minister to the life of all who read these words. I pray that this book will be of great help in their spiritual growth. I ask you, beloved reader, to be very open-minded while you read and although you may not identify with some of the things that read, I trust that someone will be touched by the power of the Holy Spirit and understand that he is not alone in the midst of his anguish.

The subject at hand is an abnormal feeling of pain and sorrow that develops into a spirit of anguish. It is not simply feeling distressed—instead, it is a feeling that lingers and hinders our walk with the Lord. Symptoms of anguish include complaining, disagreements, crying, self-pity, neglect of oneself, others, and responsibilities, and many others. Some people choose complete silence when they're in anguish, separating and isolating themselves from everything around them. The person who is being tormented by this spirit feels that only he or she has gone through this or that situation and that nobody understands them. Distress can be the result of repressed anger, lack of forgiveness of ourselves and others. It is also often great sorrow for maltreatment or abuse suffered in childhood or even as adults. It is worth noting that it is a proven fact that many of the internal conflicts that bring about anguish are due to a myriad of bad decisions that we have taken over the course of our lives. Many people have fallen under a spirit of anguish when they have found themselves at a crossroads and, without thinking, have made decisions and taken actions that had disastrous consequences on themselves and their families.

Many of these people have been medically diagnosed as depressed. Some take medications that have side-effects, such as anti-depressants. These help them not only to stay calm but also to sleep. There is no definite pattern as to how someone falls under a spirit of anguish, but I am sure that within these pages, people will have the opportunity to be set free as they enter into routine obedience to God and cry out: "Deliver me from my anguish, Lord!"

If you want to learn more about this topic, then I invite you to continue reading and to prepare to dive deeply into the powerful

Word of God. In the following pages, we will unearth many Biblical treasures that will transform the way people think about and adapt to the things that happen in their everyday lives.

When I was a child, my mother told me a story about a woman who had a husband and a young son. One day, her husband was called to the battlefront of the Vietnam War. Not long after he left, soldiers came to the woman's home to give her the news that her husband had died in combat. It didn't take very long when they called her only child to report to military duty. That mother was left totally alone. She did not have anyone else, and the only things she had were taken from her. She cried without consolation at her husband's death and the absence of her child. It wasn't long after her son departed, when two soldiers knocked on the door to give her the bad news that her son had also died in combat. The news was devastating for the mother. She felt desperate. According to the story, when she learned of this second loss, she ran down the street toward a bus stop. Her anguish was so great that it caused her to lose her reasoning and she never returned home. All her neighbors would see her sitting under a tree at the bus stop, as if she were waiting for someone. When someone asked what she was doing there, she would say she was waiting for her husband and her son who would soon return from the war. Time passed and she remained sitting under the tree, many times crying and talking to herself. Children in the neighborhood called her crazy. She only looked at them and smiled as she waited for the bus quietly. She remained under the tree day and night until she became ill, dying of melancholy and sadness. Although

I don't know the veracity of this story, I am astonished to see how this woman lost her desire to live at the loss of her loved ones.

It is interesting to watch people deal with adversity in many different ways. The economic situation in this world, for example, has affected everyone, rich and poor, young and old, large and small. We have all been affected by the world's financial disaster in some way, shape or fashion—some to a greater extent than others. Nonetheless, no one can say that they have not been affected, directly or indirectly, by the economic and social changes we face today. We cannot deny this reality: These changes cause distress in both men and women.

I recently read a news story that cited a great increase in the number of suicides due to the condition of the global economy. If we survey passers-by whether they have ever had any anguish, sorrow, pain, disappointment, or any other sadness, I can assure you that everyone would have something to contribute. This is part of being human and living in this world. There are situations or things that we can anticipate and avoid. But other things are inevitable, usually taking us by surprise. Emotional crises can touch all aspects of a person's life, especially if the person does not have their faith on the immovable rock of ages, which is Jesus Christ. Some people are so strong that when they go through tribulations and disappointments, they are stronger. Others hide their emotions for months and even years, even to the grave because they never expressed what they were feeling, preferring silence until death. Many others feel continuous anguish stemming from some event in their lives, but choose to walk through life as if nothing ever happened.

These people attempt to shut off their feelings and pain as a Pandora's Box; they will never face reality. However, other people become so fragile that in the midst of their situation, their lives comes to a total halt, preventing them from living their lives to the fullest, as the story I told earlier. It is possible that many times we have left the doors open, welcoming a spirit of anguish to enter our lives. Once it has entered, it can be concealed for some time but begins to manifest itself in different ways. Anguish is visible on the faces of many people; they are loaded with great sadness and bitterness. The majority of people who experience anguish eventually are diagnosed with depression.

Though it may be hard to believe, many of the people who are being oppressed by a spirit of anguish are not only believers in the Lord but also within our congregations. They interact and participate in church activities and fellowship with other believers as if nothing were happening to them. Upon initial observation, it might seem they are very happy, but oftentimes it is simply a mask. If you look at them closely, you would see the pain in their profound gaze. We see their faces but we know not their hearts. Many people lead a lonely life because they feel claustrophobic when they're with others. They are also very introverted and untrusting. However, I have found that when I open my heart to them, they begin to open their heart to tell me their story and pain. Some people do not like to listen to others' problems because they are not adequately prepared, have little time, or are tired of listening to the person's ongoing complaints and crying. As a result, they step away from the person because the person is "hopeless." The only way a person can patiently listen and help the distressed person to be truly free is by letting the Holy Spirit use them, asking for wisdom, and shining the light of God's word on all their thoughts. According to doctors, depression is as dangerous as a heart attack. I have heard that for many people, depression is a time bomb, which, when it explodes, does great harm, not only to the one who is suffering but also to the innocent bystanders around them. It is very important to identify this spirit so we can confront it and find a way for the person to be free before it produces greater damage—not only in them but also for those around them.

Opening the Doors of my Heart

From a very early age, I liked writing. Although I have never published any of my writings, God has allowed me to write several poems and songs which are very close to my heart. I always dreamed about writing a book someday. Although sometimes I would begin writing, for some reason, I could never finish. It seems that the times that I began to write, something would happen to keep me from continuing. My last attempt at writing was an autobiography, which was almost complete. I didn't feel totally happy with the content of the manuscript, but I thought that someday I would publish it—when I was ready. One day, my computer crashed, and I lost everything, including my book. I did not think it a great loss.

I must confess that I never imagined God would have me write about the topic in this book—anguish. But God's ways are not ours. In obedience to God, I began speaking on the topic of anguish, which is a very real condition in the world today.

At the beginning of the 1970s, unexpected things emerged in our home. Who would have imagined the course of our lives would be completely changed by a bad decision from a single member of the family? As a result of the situation that was going on with my parents, some of us—mere children—were affected emotionally. We cried all day because we did not know what would happen to our family. For the older children, it seemed as if our world was falling apart before our eyes. We felt helpless. One day, when we least expected, my father decided to send my sister Vilma and me from Puerto Rico to La Grange, Illinois, to live with our aunt to get away from the difficult situation for a while. I will never forget this experience. My environment was changed from one day to another, and I could do nothing to avoid it. We were teenagers—uprooted as a plant pulled from the earth—our world—to go to a place completely unknown, far away from our family and our friends. To top it off, we were now to speak another language—one we did not know.

To my recollection, this was the first time I was directly affected by a spirit of anguish. Because I did not speak the language, I understood very little of what was taught in school. I felt great frustration. I wrote letters to my mother day after day, telling her of my sadness and how we missed them all. Many times, even without realizing it, my tears fell on the paper as I wrote. Later on, I learned that because of our separation, every time my mother received one of my letters, she would cry. The void was intense; the nights were long so I took refuge in writing. At that time, I also wrote my feelings in a journal. I spent much time imagining that I was in Puerto Rico and dreamed of one day returning to live and to finish my studies on the island. That day never came because months later, my father decided to move to Florida and sent us tickets to meet them there—settling for the rest of our lives until we were old enough to decide for ourselves. In spite of all the negative feelings I had felt during the previous months, something good resulted of that abrupt shift. Without realizing it, I overcame the feeling of anguish and resumed the course of my life. I continued to study and learned to dominate the monster that caused me so much fear—the English language. As an adult, God has given me the opportunity to go back to visit the island many times and enjoy a nice vacation with friends and family. I can testify today that God never left my side while in the midst of that anguish. In time, I realized that God's divine plans led to blessings in my life.

Anguish does not discriminate by age. Many young people experience anguish and many times, nobody around them realizes this. It is possible that a problem that may seem simple for an adult will prove to be something catastrophic for a young man or woman. Maintaining open communication is of vital importance in the family circle. If a family closes the channels of communication, especially between parents and children, it is possible that the young one will look to express their feelings in other forms, some of which may not be appropriate. This is the reason many succumb to depression and others resort to alcohol, drugs, pornography, and many other things more that are not pleasant in the eyes of God. Each father and mother should be aware of what happens in the life of their children, especially at puberty and adolescence. This is a very dangerous stage, which Satan uses to destroy the tender lives of many young people, many of whom are so overcome and blinded by their anguish that they attempt suicide. Because I was raised in a Christian home, we learned values and appropriate behavior for the family of a pastor. When faced with a spirit of anguish throughout my life, I have learned to trust and hope in the Lord, and God has given me the strength to overcome in the midst of my situation and move forward to face the next challenge.

When my sister and I sang together as young girls, we were known as "The Velázquez Sisters." We would go with our parents to sing at church activities—whether for ministers, ladies, men, teens, and children. I remember my mother admonishing us that any time we were invited to sing we should take time to pray and read the Word so that God would use us for His glory. Seeking God before ministering to others was what made the difference between two ordinary girls and us. I remember my mother being happy when we memorized Bible verses. She made sure we were rewarded when we recited a Psalm from memory. These are some of the things that have made me the woman I am today. In all these years I have understood that when the Word of God is sown in the heart of a child, it never returns void. At the precise moment, it will do the work for which it has been sent. In my walk through this world, in a moment of spiritual carelessness, I have diverted a little from the path of the Lord, but when I felt lost and vulnerable. I was able to rely on the Word that was sown in my heart throughout my childhood. It became Rhema and has been the tool that has sustained me and has allowed me get up time and time again.

The Spirit of Anguish has Always Existed

If we look at the Scriptures, we will find that this spirit has been attacking humans since the beginning of times. Many of the great men and women of God had moments where they felt threatened by defeat and fear. However, these periods of distress did not lead them to the point of falling into depression, because they cried out to God and were soon delivered and moved on. Many Christians, however, nurture the spirit of anguish when it knocks on their door. They begin to harbor feelings of negativity, guilt, bitterness, resentment, self-pity, and self-punishment. As more time passes by, the more that this feeling continues to control the inner man, the more it undermines our spiritual life. If it is not corrected in time, this feeling can become a spirit of anguish. Then it becomes oppression. Later on, it turns into depression and, in many cases it reaches to the point of possession, which is the last mental and spiritual state that can lead a person to total madness. It is of vital importance to pay close attention to these symptoms throughout this process. Just as our spiritual growth is a silent process, so is the work of Satan because if we do not identify it and discard it in time from our inner being, it will progress gradually until it reaches its final goal which is to lead men to destruction and eternal damnation.

The people of Israel found themselves many times in the midst of anguish where they felt that God had abandoned them. They displayed their anguish by complaining continuously and longing for the things they had left behind in Egypt. But when we look at the root of the problems that arose, we realize that these situations came as a result of the disobedience of having given their back to God and turning to other gods. However, we may note that once they cried out to God, they were delivered. God always gave them a way out of their situation. We can see a first example, in Exodus 3:7- 9. At that time the people of God were slaves in Egypt. The more the Egyptians oppressed them, the more the Israelites multiplied and grew in a way that the Egyptians feared them. The Egyptians increased their burdens with heavy labor and kept their lives in bondage. In the midst of this great oppression, God called a man named Moses who later became the leader that God used as his instrument to deliver his people from the land of slavery to the land of freedom, the promised land. God brought His people out of bondage with a strong arm, showing His power and love towards them. It didn't take long after having crossed the Red Sea that they began to feel bad and complain against Moses. They witnessed how God brought them out from under Pharaoh's oppression with a strong arm. However, with each opportunity, they reminisced and longed for the food in Egypt, forgetting about the great anguish and oppression that they had lived in for so many years. They are a portrait of many of us believers. We forget where God pulled us from, and we begin to yearn for the things that we had in the world. The result of bad decisions is also often the cause of constant anguish in many people, since the enemy takes advantage of this to accuse us constantly.

In that same line of thoughts, let us look at chapter 4 of Deuteronomy. In this chapter, God through Moses directly appealed to the people to obedience, calling them to reflect on the things that the Lord their God had done for them. In verse 15, God continued speaking and warning his people against the idolatry. However, in His immense love and mercy, He said in verses 30-31: When thou art in tribulation, and all these things are come upon thee, even in the latter days, if thou turn to the LORD thy God, and shall be obedient unto his voice; (For the LORD thy God is a merciful God;) he will not forsake thee, neither destroy thee, nor forget the covenant of thy fathers which he swore unto them.

God is a god of covenant. He likes dealing with us directly and personally. Unfortunately, at some time in our lives, the vast majority of us have failed. We have disobeyed God's voice, and we have strayed from his precepts. But God does not dwell on what you and I have done. No matter our condition, His love never leaves us. Better yet, when we felt alone, He was closer to us, without our realizing it. If we believe not, yet He abides faithful; He cannot deny himself (2 Timothy 2:13).

The Spirit of Anguish has Always Existed

There was a time in my life that God had to deal with me in a similar manner. Due to circumstances in my life, I had strayed away from God for some time. I had wasted several years of my life in sin, making wrong decisions, grieving God and running from the things of God. After I returned to the ways of the Lord, things were not the same as before. I didn't feel the joy of salvation within me, because now the feeling of guilt and pain caused me great anguish. This spirit of anguish seized me in such a way that I could not hear the voice of God. I could not hear the message when it was being preached nor could I memorize the praise and worship songs. I noticed that as soon as I came through the doors of a church, I would get a headache. Many times, I spent the entire service crying without understanding why. All the people who tried to get close to me would not stay around me very long because they would get tired of listening to me and my regrets about what had happened in my past when I turned my back on the Lord and offended Him in myriad ways. I always ended up crying. This crying was not because I felt the presence of God in my life; rather, it was from the anguish that consumed me. It was a deep sense of guilt for having left the Lord. Time and again, I would tell others of how God ministered through me and how I disappointed Him.

One day, my brother Miguel invited me to a church to hear a well-known Christian singer, Harry Maldonado. After having preached, Harry started the altar call. He looked toward where I was sitting and asked me to come forward. Once at the altar, God began to minister to my life through his servant, as if he had known me all along. God revealed to him all what I gone through and he told me that despite everything that had happened, God was going to restore me and that "the glory of this latter house shall be greater than of the former, saith the LORD of hosts: Haggai 2:9."

There was no major change in my life at that time. I was always looking for a "scapegoat" in order to justify my alienation from God. The excuses were as layers of protection that I had created for myself so that nobody would confront me with the facts and shake me out of my hollow spiritual litany. I felt like that prodigal son, who once he returned to his home asked that his father would have him only as one of his workers—not his son. Faced with this situation, the enemy took advantage of my life. I had no happiness and freedom. So I kept quiet sitting in the pews without doing anything for the Lord.

One Sunday afternoon in 2005, while in the church service where I started congregating, we had a minister of God from Puerto Rico visit us—a woman. After she preached, she called me to the front to pray for me. From the moment she called me, I started to cry. My knees were shaking at the thought that God would speak to me again, and I still didn't feel ready to leave my comfort zone. I listened to her pray for me as she rebuked the spirit of anguish in my life. God began talking through her said that he was drying my tears of sorrow, and removing all spirit of anguish so that he tears that pour out from my eyes from now on will be of happiness and joy when I felt His presence. While the preacher wiped away those tears of anguish of my cheeks, I felt a great burden was lifted from my shoulders. What was striking to me was that she finished ministering to me by saying: "and the glory of the latter house shall be greater than the former." Today I can say with all sincerity: Thank you, God—that I can talk to others and testify what Christ did for me and where he pulled me from without feeling overwhelmed by that spirit of anguish. To feel freedom from that oppression of the spirit of anguish makes me want to serve my God and rejoice before His presence all the time. Today I feel that I am more in love with my God than ever before.

The word of God says in 2 Corinthians 5:17; so that if any man be in Christ, he is a new creature; old things have passed away; behold all things are become new. One of my favorite expressions is that God is a God of opportunity and new beginnings. The sad thing is that many times we come to the Lord and do not want to drop the heavy burden of our past that causes us anguish and sorrow. In most cases, although we have asked God for forgiveness, we have not yet forgiven ourselves. Isaiah 43:25 says: I, even I, am he that blotted out thy transgressions for mine own sake, and will not remember thy sins. To live a happy and victorious life in Christ Jesus, interior healing is far more important than anything else. Micah 7:19 says: He will turn again, he will have compassion upon us; he will subdue our iniquities; and thou wilt cast all their sins into the depths of the sea.

Anguish as a Result of Our Trials

I was totally shocked to review statistics several years ago that indicated that the vast majority of people found in mental hospitals or mental health institutions were people who at some point in their lives had experienced the goodness of God. I was even more surprised to learn that this included many Christians who had been leaders in their churches and even pastors. The figures were overwhelming and alarmingly high because I tend to think it is almost counterintuitive that a person full of God and His Holy Spirit succumb to this. The problem is not simply being bothered or attacked; rather, it is when we allow ourselves to be seduced by this destructive spirit to the point of numbness.

There are many things that can cause distress or affliction in us as we walk through this world. In John 16:33, Jesus told his disciples that in the world we would suffer affliction. Therefore, we should not be taken by surprise when we are in times of pain, sadness and distress. A loss of one loved one, job loss, property or estate loss, divorce or other adverse situations can bring great distress and sadness to our lives. However, the believer in Christ Jesus who has been born again and who knows in whom he has believed must use these things as a

Anguish as a Result of Our Trials

stepping stones while on the way to heaven. We must always remember the famous saying: "While there is life, there is hope."

As Christians we know we have to be tested as gold. Job expressed it this way (Job 23:10): But he knows the way that I take: when he hath tried me, I shall come forth as gold. Psalm 7:9 says that God tests the mind and heart. Psalm 11:5 also says that God tests the righteous. In Psalm 17:3, the Psalmist was totally convinced that his heart had been tested by God and no wickedness was found in it. Our faith has to be tested. Recall 1 Peter 1:7: That the trial of your faith, being much more precious than of gold that perishes, though it be tried with fire, might be found unto praise and honor and glory at the appearing of Jesus Christ. In Zechariah 13:9, God says: And I will bring the third part through the fire, and will refine them as silver is refined, and will try them as gold is tried: they shall call on my name, and I will hear them: I will say, It is my people: and they shall say: The LORD is my God.

There are moments in our lives when we feel we're going through a fiery trial. Our distress is so strong that we think we will lose our minds. It is important to know the difference between when we are being tested by God or simply suffering the consequences of our disobedience. Regardless, we must know that in both cases, we expect that God will provide us with a way out.1 Corinthians 3:13 says: Every man's work shall be made manifest: for the day shall declare it, because it shall be revealed by fire; and the fire shall try every man's work of what sort it is. But there is beatitude for those who pass the test. James 1:2-3 tells us something that to the mind of any human being seems absurd but it is real: "My brethren, count it all joy when ye fall into diverse temptations; knowing this, that the trying of your faith works patience." James 1:12 goes on to say: "Blessed is the man that endures temptation: for when he is tried, he shall receive the crown of life, which the Lord hath promised to them that love him." True believers do not faint in the midst of testing. The Apostle Paul, in the midst of trials, continued to urge the Ephesian church to persevere. Ephesians 3:13: "Wherefore I desire that ye faint not at my tribulations for you, which is your glory." Hebrews 12:5 says, "And ye have forgotten the exhortation which speaks unto you as unto children, "My son, despise not thou the chastening of the Lord, nor faint when thou art rebuked of him." David experienced the trial and also punishment when he had disobeyed God, but deep within his heart he had such a pure feeling of love for God. In Psalm 94, verse 12 says: "Blessed is the man whom thou chasten, O LORD, and teaches him out of thy law." Isaiah 48:10 says: "Behold, I have refined thee, but not with silver; I have chosen thee in the furnace of affliction." That is, no matter if you think you're going through the bitterest times in your life; right there in the oven of affliction, God wants to glorify himself in your life. He entered into the fiery furnace with Shadrach, Meshach and Abednego. In Daniel Chapter 3, they were tied up a furnace that was heated seven times more than usual. When King Nebuchadnezzar inspected the furnace the following day, he found four men walking around in the middle of the fire. Likewise, God promises to go inside and walk around in the fire with us, untied and without getting burned, if you are faithful to Him even in the midst of trials.

There are promises of God that you must remember when you are in these moments of anguish. Isaiah 43:2 says, "When thou passest through the waters, I will be with thee; and through the rivers, they shall not overflow thee: when thou walkest through the fire, thou shalt not be burned; neither shall the flame kindle upon thee." 1 Peter 4:12-14 says: "Beloved, think it not strange concerning the fiery trial which is to try you, as though some strange thing happened unto you: But rejoice, inasmuch as ye are partakers of Christ's sufferings; that, when his glory shall be revealed, ye may be glad also with exceeding joy. If ye be reproached for the name of Christ, happy are ye; for the spirit of glory and of God resteth upon you: on their part he is evil spoken of, but on your part he is glorified."

It All Starts In Your Mind

Imagine that your brain is a computer with several functions. On the desktop of this computer, there are some icons that represent various functions. It also has a hard drive that is called "the memory." Within this memory, there are two categories, active or current files and past memory or filed items. Once you spend some time on your files, these are processed and saved to the hard drive memory.

Within the human brain there are two sections of memory as well, bad memories and good memories. Too often, there are unfiled records in our minds. There are also some records or memories that are shuffled from side to side in our minds. These files are memories of the past we do not want to delete and although they are of no good use, we keep holding on to them. These memories take away our peace and quietness of spirit; they are tools used by the "spirit of distress or anguish" to torment us. By keeping those thoughts active in our mind, we are unable to focus on the present because our mind is too busy ruminating and reliving the past. When this happens in a Christian, the enemy takes advantage of the situation and does not allow them to move forward. This is what we see when a person changes and succumbs to deeps thoughts. James 1:8 says the double minded man is unstable in all his ways. It is being manipulated by the spirit of anxiety and has not realized its spiritual state. Another potential situation is when people tend to be very cautious and controlling. These are people that want to make sure they cover all the bases and do not leave room for God to take control of their lives and their problems. These people often fall into distress and worry about things that have not yet happened and things that may never happen.

Thoughts are the activity and creation of the mind; said of everything that is brought into existence through intellectual activity. The Christian who keeps their mind on the things of God has victory. So the Apostle Paul exhorts us in Philippians 4:8, saying, brethren, whatever is true, whatever honest, whatsoever things are just, whatever is pure, whatever is lovely, whatever is admirable-if there is any virtue and if any praise, think on these things.

May times we want to hide and not bring to light many things that we must bring out so we can be totally free of that sense of guilt that continuously harasses us and brings great distress. God knows our thoughts—there is nothing hidden from his eyes. Jeremiah 17:10 says I the LORD search the heart, I try the reins, even to give every man according to his ways, and according to the fruit of his doings. The men and women of God must be transparent at all times and should express themselves as the psalmist David in Psalms 139:23, "Search me, o God, and know my heart; Try me and know my thoughts." Whenever negative thoughts enter your mind, remember 2 Corinthians 10:5, "Casting down imaginations, and every high thing that exalted itself against the knowledge of God, and bringing into captivity every thought to the obedience of Christ." In John 1:48 when Jesus converses with Nathanael as he marvels and asks where Jesus knew him from, Jesus replied that, prior to Philip calling him, as he was under the fig tree, Jesus knew him. Nathanael had made a negative comment when Philip told him of Jesus. Little did he know Jesus had heard his conversation with Philip prior to his being called. The truth of the matter is that before our bones were formed in the womb of our mother, God already knew us and had a plan designed for our life. The Bible says that if any man loves God, he is known by him. God knows our inner being, our journey, our lives, and even our most profound dreams. 2 Timothy 2:19 tells us: "Nevertheless the foundation of God standeth sure, having this seal: The Lord knoweth them that are his. And, Let every one that nameth the name of Christ depart from iniquity." If God knows us so well, I wonder: Why is it that it is often so difficult to come before him in prayer—to open our hearts and allow him to come and deliver us from anguish? The Bible says in Revelation 12:10 that Satan accuses God's children day and night in front of our God. That is why many people cannot be delivered from that sense of guilt that harasses them. When we are tormented by bad memories, we must recognize that this is simply a weapon used by the enemy to take away the peace and joy that God wants to bring into our lives.

It is important that you understand that this way of thinking—or even feelings of bitterness—is not of God. These are chains that the

It All Starts In Your Mind

enemy has placed in your life. You will live a life of defeat, great sadness, and despair unless you realize that Jesus wants to set you free of your anguish. We cannot spend minutes entertaining negative thoughts that may cause us harm. You and I—brother and sister in Christ—must renew our minds day by day. Ephesians 4:23 tells us to be renewed in the spirit of our minds. Romans 12:2 says, "And be not conformed to this world: but be ye transformed by the renewing of your mind, that ye may prove what is that good, and acceptable, and perfect, will of God." Colossians 3:10 says, "And have put on the new man, which is renewed in knowledge after the image of him that created him." God did not created us to be slaves of our bad thoughts and memories. He wants his children to be free to fulfill His divine purpose.

Genesis 37 tells a story well known for many of us, the story of Joseph. This young man was sold to the Ishmaelites by his brothers because they were envious of him. They even made his father believe that their brother was dead. This caused great distress to Jacob, who believed what his sons said and vowed to mourn his son to the grave. Behind it all, God had a plan for his people.

Many times we do not understand why we go through certain things and begin to question God. As we follow the story of Joseph, we see that he was brought to Egypt, where he was sold to Potiphar, an officer of Pharaoh, captain of the guard. Later we see that the wife of Potiphar tried to seduce Joseph, and he fled. When this happened, the angry woman accused him of wanting to abuse her, and he was sent to prison. While in prison, Joseph interpreted two dreams, one to the butler and one to the baker, respectively. Both men were in prison with him. Both of these dreams came to pass and the baker died as he had dreamed and the chief butler was restored to his position in the kingdom. When the chief butler was set free, according to Joseph's interpretation, he totally forgot he had made a promise to Joseph, who was still a prisoner that he would plead for him before Pharaoh. This man chose not to remember the bad experience of his imprisonment and in doing so, he forgot about Joseph as well. But oh how good it is to know that God does not forget. One day, when Pharaoh had a dream and found no one to interpret it, this man's memory was activated and he felt very bad about not keeping his word. Taking advantage of the situation, he made mention of the young Hebrew and later, Joseph was released to find grace in the eyes of Pharaoh. Those moments of anguish that Joseph suffered were permitted by God so that later he could bless his own family. God's purpose was fulfilled. If a word of God has been unleashed upon your life, God will make it happen. No matter how long it has been or how long it may take, it will come to pass. For the vision is yet for an appointed time, but at the end it shall speak, and not lie: though it tarry, wait for it; because it will surely come, it will not tarry (Habakkuk 2:3).

God used to remind his people of their hardness of heart: "Remember, do not forget that you have provoked the wrath of LORD thy God in the wilderness since the day you left the land of Egypt, until ye came into this place, you have been rebellious against the Lord"

(Deuteronomy 9:7). In the same chapter, God continued to remind his people Israel of all He had done for them and of their disobedience.

The Psalmist David activated his memories in Psalm 51:3: "For I know my transgressions and my sin is ever before me." David was aware that he had failed God and these memories caused him great distress. When Peter denied Jesus, his memory was activated (Mark 14:72), but it was not until he had denied Jesus for the third time that he remembered the words spoken by Jesus himself when he said, "Before the cock crows twice, thou shalt deny me three times."

Then the Bible goes on to say that thinking about this (Peter), he wept. Just imagine how these words echoed in his mind over and over. The sad case is that our memory often fails to act in time to help us avoid many tears and much pain.

Five spiritual forces can be considered principalities or kingdoms and can appear at any given time in our lives. Reviewing the story in Joshua chapter 10, we see five kings that came together against the people of God. These kings were: Adonisec King of Jerusalem, Hohan the king of Hebron, Piram king of Jerimoth, Japhia king of Lachish, and Debit king of Eglon. There are moments in our lives when it seems like we are bombarded by problems all at once and we say, "This was the last thing I needed." The Bible clearly states in Ephesians 6:12: "For we wrestle not against flesh and blood, but against principalities, against powers, against the rulers of the darkness of this world, against spiritual wickedness in high places."

Each of these kings symbolizes different situations we face in our life—both on a daily level and at a spiritual level:

1. **Adonisec (Jerusalem)** represents situations involving legal problems and issues that have to do with justice, such as immigration. This spirit also manifests itself in discrimination and segregation. It speaks of feeling defenseless against the arrogance of someone in authority and being easily intimidated. This spirit causes depression and oppression.

2. **Hohan (king of Hebron)** means uncertain or significant doubt. This spirit is manifested when our faith is weakened and we begin to think that that we may not be in the truth. It speaks of questioning our faith and all that we previously defended with courage. This spirit also lowers our self esteem. Satan is an expert to create doubt in the mind of man, and he knows that once this happens, our faith is weakened and we are led into a spirit of religiosity.

3. **Piran (king of Jarmuth): Heb. Pyramus, "wild beast."** This is an aggressive spirit. It does not know order or rules and will not submit to anyone. It evidences itself in disease, violence, tragedies, and moments of despair. It speaks of things falling apart. This is also a spirit of frustration and discouragement.

4. **Japhia (king of Lachish). Yafi, "he shines" or "Brilliant [splendid, sparkling]."**

Pride, one who wants all the attention and believes he is better than anyone. It's when we start to look at everything the world offers and divert our eyes off God. It focuses on wealth and earthly things. We become anxious because we wish for certain things, but we cannot get them. We look to other sources to obtain what we want. It speaks of taking our dependence off God trusting in our own strength. This spirit causes spiritual blindness, darkness, or lack of disclosure.

5. 5) **Debir (King of Eglon): Heb. Debir Debir and Debîrâh,** means "what is behind," "oracle," the hidden things. Also means "Two faces." This is the spirit that is always looking to bring discord among brethren. It manifests itself in the betrayal of a friend or a brother, hypocrisy from whom we least expect, when we are deceived or when we are hypocrites with others. This is an accuser spirit.

If you study this story in this chapter, you will see that Joshua knew in whom he had firmly believed and in who had called him. God gave Joshua victory over those five kings. Joshua claimed the words that God had spoken into his life, saying: "Be not afraid of them, for I have given into your hand, and none of them will stand before you." God promised Joshua victory, and he walked on that word. It is possible that you find yourself identifying with one or more of those kings who rose against the people of God. The most important thing to remember is that no matter the situation, rest assured that if we faint not, God will see us through.

We Are Members of One Body

You may be one of those people who have done very well in life. Perhaps you are wondering how all this may apply to you. God has given each of us certain abilities, strengths and gifts that we use to work together for the growth of the kingdom. As a body, we have many members, and each of them has a function, so we, being many, are the body of Christ and individually members one of another. 1 Corinthians 6:15 asks us a question: "Know ye not that your bodies are the members of Christ? Shall I then take the members of Christ, and make them the members of a harlot? God forbid." Reading on in the same book, chapter 12 verses 11-12, "All these are the work of one and the same Spirit, and he gives them to each one, just as he determines. The body is a unit, though it is made up of many parts; and though all its parts are many, they form one body. So it is with Christ." That same biblical passage, elaborates more on this subject. God has placed each member in the body as he wanted. Those members who appear to be weaker are most necessary. Therefore we can not allow ourselves to feel that we do not contribute anything in God's plan for His Church. God did it all with purpose, and there should be unity in the members to work in harmony and complement each other for the healthy functioning of the body of Christ.

God cares deeply about the unity of his people. 1 Corinthians 1:10 says, "Now I beseech you, brethren, the name of our Lord Jesus Christ, who speak all the same thing, and not among you divisions, but that ye be perfectly joined together in one mind and one judgment." A church where members are not working properly on their responsibilities is a sick church—not a normal church. That church is in need of healing by the divine doctor. So if one member suffers, all members are affected. If a member hurts, the whole body feels pain. But when one member is honored, all members rejoice with the rest of the body. 1 Corinthians 1:13 says, "Is Christ divided? In Christ we are one, there is neither Jew nor Greek, there is no bond nor free, there is neither male nor female: for ye are all one in Christ Jesus" (Gal. 3:28).

When a person who is a member of the church body is being oppressed by the spirit of distress, he is ill and needs healing. This not only affects him or her but the whole congregation. That is why it's important we seek healing for that member of the body. Paul wrote to the Ephesians as he reminded them of the importance of unity, saying: "Till we all come in the unity of the faith, and of the knowledge of the Son of God, unto a perfect man, unto the measure of the stature of the fullness of Christ" (Ephesians 4:13). Then he goes on to say in verse 16: "From whom the whole body fitly joined together and compacted by that which every joint supplies, according to the effectual working in the measure of every part, makes increase of the body unto the edifying of itself in love." That means that as a body, we are also called to grow in every way. A growing body is not a healthy body if there is something wrong in it that is preventing its growth. Unity and harmony of all the members of the body are essential elements for conquering our spiritual battle.

In the book of Judges, chapter 20 God's people had to face a battle: "Then all the children of Israel went out, and the congregation was gathered together as one man, from Dan even to Beersheba, with the land of Gilead, unto the LORD in Mizpeh." This positive attitude and unity was what led the people to victory. Unfortunately, with all the things we have to do each day, we often fall into a stress and have no time to help each other. Everyone works with a separate agenda. Let me tell you a secret: The only way you will be able to leave the stress and mental and physical exhaustion in which we tend to fall is to start helping others less fortunate that are in some sort of need. When your heads rest on your pillow each night, you will feel the rest you have been looking for because you have understood the principle that we were created to serve others.

It Is Not a Sin to Feel Momentary Anguish

I want to make it very clear that anguish is not a sin and that anyone at any given moment is bound to experience anguish. However, we cannot nurture those moments of anguish, and we should not let ourselves be controlled by a "spirit of anguish." The following examples will reveal the difference between the two. Jesus said: "In the world you will suffer tribulations, but be of good cheer; I have overcome the world." The word speaks to us about the two men who built their houses, one built it on the sand and the other built his house on the rock. Later both of these houses were hit by a great storm, but only the one that was founded on the rock remained without collapse. The story also tells us that there came winds, rivers, and rain against both of these houses. These three elements mean that both houses were pounded by all sides, rivers whipped from below, rain from above and winds on all sides. The Christian must be that house which is built on the rock that is Christ Jesus. This is the only guarantee that we have as Christians: When we are flogged by the storms of this world, we must stand firmly, for God has promised us victory and He will not let us fall.

It Is Not a Sin to Feel Momentary Anguish

Many men and women of the Bible, which are talked about even today for their great deeds, in a given moment felt anguish and disappointment in their lives. We see the story of Moses, the great Hebrew leader that I mentioned previously. In Chapter 11 of the book of Numbers, the people of Israel started to complain directly "into God's ears" because they were tired of eating manna and wanted to eat meat. This complaint ignited the wrath of God upon them in such a way that God lit on fire one side of the campground. The people cried to Moses, and Moses cried out to the Lord. The fire was extinguished, but the people continued complaining. They wanted to eat meat.

In verses 11 to 15, Moses very distressed with this situation; he cried and complained to God. God then responded to the cries of his servant and sent quail for His people to eat. They had God on their side, as their supreme leader, but they were in constant anguish, as evidenced by their complaining to Moses. Not much time had elapsed when the people of God entered the Promised Land under the direction of Joshua. Discouragement and anxiety set in once again. God had promised to Joshua that, as he was with Moses, he would also be with him. As we look at this story, we see that God had given strict instructions against taking things from the enemy's camp in Joshua 6:17-19. However, a man named Achan was overcome by ambition and hid a block of forbidden gold, causing the wrath of God to burn against Israel. This disobedience brought about disastrous consequences, since all the men that went up against Hai were killed with their sword. Joshua then felt great anguish and disappointment and cried out to God (Joshua 7:7-9). Joshua felt completely helpless to the point of desiring that he was dead. God then revealed Achan's sin to Joshua.

I would like to remind you that it was not Joshua who had sinned. But this irresponsible act of one individual caused chaos among the people. Many times, the sin of disobedience—either our own or other people's—can lead us to the point of the anguish and despair. It is important that we make sure there are no forbidden things in our lives such as sin or disobedience that is causing us to be defeated or holding back the blessings of God.

Another example is the prophet Elijah—a man with unique power of which we often hear preached. Although he was used by God in doing wonderful things, he also had moments of anguish and despair. In 1 Kings Chapter 17, Elijah had no fear when he presented himself in front of King Ahab to predict a great drought. During that time, based on God's orders, he settled near a brook named Cherith. There, God provided bread and meat twice a day, and he drank water from the stream. After a few days, the stream became dry due to lack of rain. God instructed him to go to Zarephath of Sidon where God already had a widow prepared to support him. Later, Elijah was filled with the power of God defying the prophets of Baal.

One of the things that strikes me about this great man of God is the courage with which he faced four hundred and fifty prophets of Baal. He felt total security that their god would not respond. He

It Is Not a Sin to Feel Momentary Anguish

even dared to make a mockery of them when they cried out to their god. In this amazing story, he ends up killing all the prophets of Baal as they did not receive the response from their god. God sent fire from heaven and consumed Elijah's offering, even the drops of water that had been placed in the ditches around it. After this great victory, Elijah returned to King Ahab to advise him that God was going to send rain as an answer to his prayers.

It didn't take long for the news that Elijah had killed the prophets of Baal to reach the ears of an evil woman named Jezebel. This woman sent a messenger to Elijah with death threats. In 1 Kings 19:3, the Bible says that seeing the danger, Elijah got up and went to save his life. He was in the desert one day when he came upon a juniper tree. He wished he were dead: "I've had enough, O Lord, take my life, for I am not better than my parents."

In this chapter we can clearly see the human side of Elijah when he felt totally intimidated by a simple woman who threatened his life. Yes, it was the same man who had just put to death 450 prophets of Baal. Now he was facing anguish and despair. This tells us that it is not a sin to feel distressed. Physically, Elijah was exhausted and fell asleep quickly. God sent an angel with food and water to refresh him, but Elijah was very tired and went back to sleep. Again the angel awoke him with food and told him to get up and eat because he had a long road ahead. This meal kept him forty days and forty nights.

Although God was giving him strength, the first thing he did upon arriving at Horeb was to hide in a cave. This is precisely what we do many times, even when God is dealing with us. Anxiety and fear startle us and don't allow us to see that God has everything under control. Right there in the cave, he received a word from the Lord, saying: "What are you doing here, Elijah?" It is not that God ignored his situation; God knew perfectly well what happened to Elijah, but He was giving Elijah an opportunity to vent. Let us note that, despite everything Elijah told God, God did not seem to pay attention because He already had another plan for Elijah. It was not the time to complain or stop along the way. God told him to stand outside the cave, in front of the mountain of God.

Many times we have to get out of the cave called "our comfort zone" and climb the mountain for God to give us a fresh revelation of his Word. First Elijah saw a very strong wind so powerful that it tore the mountains and shattered the rocks, but the Lord was not in the wind. After that, an earthquake, but the Lord was not in the earthquake, after the earthquake a fire, but the Lord was not in the fire. After the fire came a gentle whisper, and Elijah heard God's voice that asked him again: "What are you doing here, Elijah?" He told God what happened because he feared for his life. Regardless of everything Elijah was going through, he was obedient to the voice of God every time.

This story teaches us that it does not matter that we are going through. Although we may be in the midst of anxiety and despair, we must be connected with the Lord and be obedient to His word. In times of spiritual weakness, we must not deviate from the vision. God always has men and women ready to proceed with the work that we started.

It Is Not a Sin to Feel Momentary Anguish

That is why God wanting to promote Elijah to another dimension and place Elisha as his successor.

As Christians, when we mention the subject of anguish, one Bible character immediately comes to mind—merely because he had many moments of anguish. I am referring to the great patriarch Job. Through the ages, his story has served us as comfort and an example of a great man who, having lost everything in life including his children, could not stand waiting in that even from the dust God would lift him up. The Bible says Job was a man like none other on earth. In spite of this, he experienced a series of unspeakable tests throughout his life. In the midst of his situation, Job said, "Therefore I will not refrain my mouth; I will speak in the anguish of my spirit; I will complain in the bitterness of my soul" (Job 7:11). In chapter 10:1, he exclaimed: "My soul is weary of my life; I will leave my complaint upon myself; I will speak in the bitterness of my soul." My finite and limited mind can only imagine the great anguish that this man had in his soul. I suppose he believed that everything had ended for him. But further on in his trials, God took away his anguish and gave him great victory for having remained faithful.

Let us note the interesting thing about this story. At the beginning of this book, Satan was allowed to take away everything this man possessed—including his children. I cannot even imagine what that would be like! The Bible says in Job 1:20-21: "Then Job arose, and rent his mantle, and shaved his head, and fell down upon the ground, and worshipped, And said, Naked came I out of my mother's womb, and naked shall I return thither: the LORD gave, and the LORD hath taken away; blessed be the name of the LORD." Verse 22 goes on to say "In all this, Job sinned not, not charged God foolishly." That is to say, he understood that God had some purpose for all that had happened to him.

As we continue our tour of the Bible, I want to go back to David—the "the sweet psalmist of Israel" (2 Samuel 23:1). The boy that with a single stone defeated Goliath now exclaimed: "O my God, my soul is cast down within me: therefore will I remember thee from the land of Jordan, and of the Hermonites, from the hill Mizar" (Psalm 42:6).

The trajectory of David's life consisted of many ups and downs. The majority of his anguish and anger were caused due to his disobedience and lack of maturity. Despite all his faults, the Bible says that he was a man after God's own heart. Let's take a look at some of those moments; in 1 Chronicles 13, when it is proposed to relocate the ark of God from Kiriath-jearim, without educating himself on how to or what were the rules for transporting the ark of God, David proceeded to bring it home. God had given specific instructions that the Ark of the Covenant, as it used to be called, should be transported only by the sons of the Levites, carried on their shoulders by two bars, as the Lord commanded Moses. Thinking that he was doing the right thing, David transported the Ark in a new cart. David and all Israel rejoiced, playing before God with all their might, with singing and with harps, psalteries, timbrels, cymbals, and trumpets. When they arrived at the threshing floor of Chidon, Uzzah reached out his hand to hold the ark because

It Is Not a Sin to Feel Momentary Anguish

the oxen stumbled. God's anger burned against Uzzah, and He struck him dead. The verses that follow tell us that David felt great sadness because of this event and feared God. He then stopped to educate himself on the correct way of carrying the Ark of the Covenant. This is a great example of how anguish can come into our lives by disobedience made in ignorance.

In Chapter 16, verses 7 to 36, the situation is resolved, and David returned to give thanks to God and to worship His name. Soon thereafter, God used David to defeat the Philistines. You can't be confined by mistakes made due to your ignorance; going back to the instructions will put you in the right path and take you to victory.

Because the majority of the Psalms were written by David, let us pause to review some of them in order to see that although David was a man who feared God, the greater part of his life was full of challenges, anguish and despair. Those moments moved him to write the following Psalms. Psalm 5 is a request for protection. Psalms 6, 28, and 142 reflect prayers asking for mercy in the midst of trials. Psalms 7 and 43 are a prayer asking for vindication. Psalms 10, 55, 60, 108, and 129 are prayers asking for defeat of evil men. In Psalms 12, 64, 35, 57, 83, and 58, he prayed for help against enemies. Psalm 13 is a prayer asking for help in the midst of anguish and tribulation. Psalms 17 and 140 again are prayers asking for protection against oppressors or persecutors. Psalm 18 is a prayer asking for victory. Psalms 22 and 69 are a cry of distress and a song of hope. In Psalm 25 and 143, David prayed to God for direction, forgiveness and protection. Psalm 38 is a prayer of penitence. Psalm 41 is a prayer asking for health. In Psalm 42, the Psalmist cried out because he is thirsty for God. Psalms 51 and 80 are prayers of repentance, asking for purification and restoration. Psalm 56 is a prayer of confidence. Psalm 70 is a plea for release. Psalm 71 is a prayer of an elderly man. Psalm 86 is a plea for mercy. Psalm 88 is a prayer to be freed from death. Psalm 102 is a prayer of an anguished heart. Psalm 120 is a prayer against the deceitful tongue. Psalm 141 is a plea to be spared from evil, and Psalm 144 is a prayer for relief and prosperity.

I'm sure that you and I can identify with some of these psalms. The secret lies in the fact that although both David and all these men of God were caught in the spirit of distress, once they cried out to God in the midst of each of these adverse situations, God gave them the victory.

Another of David's moments of anguish can be found in 2 Samuel 15 when his own son rebelled against him. In the midst of his son's rebellion and other events, David went up mount Olivet, weeping as he went up to worship God. There are times when we have to crown the cost of pain and suffering with our hearts in our hands. But in the midst of the anguish, you can't stop to regret. We must continue to rise. Although our hearts may be torn, we must move on until we reach the altar of worship. Chapter 18 mentions a number of events that culminated in the death of Absalom. Again David experienced the valley of tears at the death of his son: "O my son Absalom, my son, my son, Absalom! Who would give me that I died in your place, Absalom, my son, my son! This event triggered a series of events that left David out of commission for some time. However, in Chapter 22, David once again lifted his head and offered a song of deliverance to God in gratitude for His strength and His support in the midst of his trials and tribulations.

The prophet Jeremiah is another great man of God who experienced moments of anguish throughout his ministry. He experienced so many moments of anguish that many called him, "The weeping prophet." God raised this man during the reign of Josiah, the last of the good kings, several years after captivity. Jerusalem was in ruins because of their sins. Jeremiah felt a great pain and anguish for his people. He could not even compare the past glory of Israel with their present condition. Even having received a call from God and the promise of his divine presence, Jeremiah was rejected by his neighbors (Jeremiah 11:19-21), by his own family (Jeremiah 12:6), by the priests and prophets (Jer 20:1-2), by his friends (Jeremiah 20:10); by all the people (Jeremiah 26:8), and lastly by the king himself (Jeremiah 36:23). In chapter 15, verse 10 of this book, Jeremiah was discouraged and weary: "Woe is me, my mother, that thou hast borne me a man of strife and a man of contention to the whole earth! I have neither lent on usury, nor men have lent to me on usury; yet every one of them doth curse me." The prophet was ready to abandon his ministry in chapter 20:8-11, "For since I spoke, I cried out, I cried violence and spoil; because the word of the LORD was made a reproach unto me, and a derision, daily. Then I said, I will not make mention of him, nor speak any more in his name. But his word was in mine heart as a burning fire shut up in my bones, and I was weary with forbearing, and I could not stay. For I heard the defaming of many fear on every side. Report, say they, and we will report it. All my familiars watched for my halting, saying, Peradventure he will be enticed, and we shall prevail against him, and we shall take our revenge on him. But the LORD is with me as a mighty terrible one: therefore my persecutors shall stumble, and they shall not prevail: they shall be greatly ashamed; for they shall not prosper: their everlasting confusion shall never be forgotten." I want you to treasure these words because they are a clear example of how in the midst of anguish, Jeremiah does not allow himself to remain in grief or lamentation. Instead, he recognizes the power of God in his life, taking his responsibility as a prophet of God to preach the message God had given him for his people.

It is believed that prophet Habakkuk was a director of music or singing in the temple. He was perplexed when he watched how evil people didn't appear to be punished by God. This distressed him greatly. He watched as sinful violence seemed to prevail everywhere, and evildoers were not punished. God revealed His divine plan to use the Chaldeans as the instrument against his disobedient children. To make matters worse, the prophet continued to complain and fret as he did not understand how God would use these people to punish his people. In the eyes of the prophet, it seemed like things got worse instead of improving, and it seemed like this would never end. During a shortage of food in the land, Habakkuk saw the glory of God (Habakkuk 3:3-4): "His glory covered the heavens and the earth was full of his praise. And his brightness was as the light; he had horns coming out of his hand, and there were hiding of his power". Habakkuk learned to trust in God. In Chapter 3:17-18, He expressed confidence in God: "Although the fig tree shall not blossom, neither shall fruit be in the vines; the labour of the olive shall fail, and the fields shall yield no meat; the flock shall be cut off from the fold, and there shall be no herd in the stalls: Yet I will rejoice in the LORD, I will joy in the God of my salvation." There are times in our lives that we are harassed by the enemy and we cannot understand how God allows his children to suffer. But how wonderful it is when God shows his glory in the midst of our adversity.

The Lord Jesus as he prayed in Gethsemane also experienced moments of great distress. Matthew 26:38 says he took Peter and the two sons of Zebedee and began to be sorrowful and very anguished. He turned to them and said: "My soul is exceedingly sorrowful to death." That does not mean that Jesus was in sin and that he was no longer God because he was a man. Rather, in his humanity, he felt pain because he knew the bitter cup he had to drink. This is the same Jesus that expressed in John 15:11: These things I have spoken unto you that my joy might remain in you and your joy may be full. To the carnal mind it is difficult to understand how someone can be in anguish but joyful at the same time.

What Happens When I allow the Spirit of Anguish to control me?

I want to point out and highlight three things that happen when we let the spirit of anguish control our emotions:

1) <u>The first thing that happens is that we cannot praise God</u>. The spirit of anguish takes the joy of salvation to keep us from worshipping God as He deserves. The psalmist David at a time of anguish felt imprisoned and exclaimed "Bring my soul out of prison, that I may praise thy name: the righteous shall compass me about; for thou shalt deal bountifully with me" (Psalm 142:7). In Psalm 137, young men who were taken captive to Babylon lamented. They were so anxious that they had no desire to praise God. They had hung their harps on the willows and when the men of Babylon asked them to sing and play their harps, they answered "How can we sing the Lord's song in a strange land?" There comes a time in our lives that the last thing we want to do is to sing. God made us free so we can adore him. We are the ones who put ourselves in bondage. The book of Ecclesiastes says, "Everything has its time… time to weep and a time to laugh"; however, when we are in anguish, we cannot enjoy the time of laughter when it comes. The spirit of anguish takes over our feelings and

What Happens When I allow the Spirit of Anguish to control me?

there is no room for happiness. There are many more good things and blessings that we receive from God; yet, we do not recognize them because we lose focus and are controlled by anguish. On another occasion, the Psalmist expressed: "O my God, my soul is cast down within me" (Psalm 42:6). In Psalm 51:12, he said, "Restore unto me the joy of thy salvation," and then in verse 15: "O Lord, open thou my lips; and my mouth shall shew forth thy praise."

I recently had the opportunity to come to know a woman that touched my life in a very short time. Her name was Miriam—the sister-in-law of my childhood friend and sister in Christ, Yolanda. While I was on vacation in Puerto Rico, Yolanda informed me that her sister-in-law Miriam was living in Florida. She gave me her contact information so I could visit with her upon my return to Florida. She was a cancer patient with little time to live. As soon as I could after returning to Florida, I called Miriam to come visit with her. I met her in a hospital. In anticipation of the visit, I imagined a sad woman because of her situation. I was prepared to bring a word of comfort from God's Word. I was surprised to see a woman who, according to doctors, was far gone. Instead, she had the most beautiful smile I had ever seen. She was so full of energy; it was contagious. Her face displayed an inner peace that I had never seen a person in such a condition. Miriam told me that when she was discharged from the hospital, she would devote her time to her children and grandchildren. She had the assurance of salvation because she knew that at the right time, God would call her home and she would be forever with the Lord. The months flew by. I called Miriam a few times to meet with her, but it seemed like every time I called her she was in Puerto Rico or traveling to some other place with her loved ones. In December, close to Christmas time, we finally met at a relative's house in Lakeland. We spent a beautiful afternoon talking about the Lord and life in general. She was preparing for Christmas day and was expecting all her children and grandchildren to come home. I was so excited. My husband and I decided visit her on Christmas. She was so happy. Come Christmas day, her small apartment was full with her entire family, and you could feel all the love in the air in such a small place. She enthusiastically introduced us to all those who were there. After that, we didn't get to see each other again. A few days later, I received the sad call letting us know that her health was declining rapidly. Two weeks later, she went home to be with the Lord. One of the things that I asked the Lord was to give me the same spirit that was in Miriam, so that others may see Christ in me, no matter what was going on in my life. Do you know that God is a joyous God? Zephaniah 3:17 says: "The LORD thy God in the midst of thee is mighty; he will save, he will rejoice over thee with joy; he will rest in his love, he will joy over thee with singing." Therefore he wants us to be joyous and happy. Paul exhorted us in 1 Thessalonians 5:16: "Rejoice evermore." You can't be joyful and anguished at the same time—you are either joyful or you are anguished. But God has promised us his peace in the midst of tribulations as long as we do not lose focus. Isaiah 26:3 says, "Thou wilt keep him in perfect peace, whose mind is stayed on thee: because he trusted in thee." Psalm 146:7: "The LORD turns loose the prisoners."

2) <u>The second thing that happens to us is that we cannot see that God is walking on our side</u>. When we are tormented by a spirit of anguish, we feel completely alone even when you are surrounded by people. Most of all, we do not feel the presence of God in our lives. In Luke 24, two of Jesus' disciples were on their way to a village called Emmaus after Jesus' crucifixion. They were very distressed because Jesus had died. They had forgotten that he had said that he would rise from the dead. Their eyes were veiled, so that they did not recognize Jesus when he joined them on their walk. He asked what they were talking about and why they were sad. They were so distressed that it was not until the moment when the Lord had departed from their side that they realized it was their master who had been walking alongside them. In John 8:15, the women went to the tomb where Jesus had been buried to anoint his body. They were in so much anguish they did not come to realize that the Master had risen from the dead. In verse 13, Jesus stood in front of Mary Magdalene and he said: "Women, why are you weeping? Who you are looking for?" Because of her great distress, she did not realize that she was talking to Jesus himself. When Jesus spoke her name, "Mary," she acknowledged she was in front of the Risen Christ. She recognized His voice. It is possible that God is glorifying himself in your moment of pain. He could be changing your environment into a great blessing, but you have not recognized the positive things

due to your anguish. When we are suffocating in pain and misery, we are overwhelmed by a spirit of anguish, and we cannot see the hand of God guiding our steps. Someone said that when words fail, God understands the language of tears. It is fine to cry; however, be sure your crying does not become the rule instead of the exception. The Lord is good, a stronghold in the day of trouble; and he knows those who trust in him (Nahum 1:7). The Psalmist knew that God was with him at all times and he said: "I will be glad and rejoice in thy mercy: for thou hast considered my trouble; thou hast known my soul in adversities" (Psalm 31: 7). In the popular poem, "Footprints," a person had a dream where he was sent to heaven to review the story of his life. He saw himself walking down the sand through the various scenes of his life. In each scene, he could see four footprints in the sand, which made him understand that two of the footprints in the sand belonged to Jesus who was walking by his side. During times of trials and tribulations, he noticed something that caught his attention. He discovered that in the most difficult moments of his life, he only saw two footprints in the sand. He cried out to the Lord saying: "Lord, you told me, when I met you, that you would walk with me, along the way, but during the worst moments of my life, I only see two footprints in the sand. I don't understand why you left me in the hours I needed you the most." Then the Lord fixed His gaze on the man and replied, "My dear child, I have loved you and will never abandon you even in the most difficult moments. When you saw that there were only two footprints in the sand was precisely in those times when I carried you in my arms." Another illustrative story is found in Matthew 8:23. Jesus entered into a boat with his disciples and fell asleep. Then, there was raised a great storm in the sea that the waves covered the boat. The disciples began to tremble and cried out to Jesus, "Lord, deliver us; we are perishing!" Then he got up and rebuked the winds and the sea and there was great calm. The disciples did not realize that Jesus was in the boat, and they became anguished as the storm increased. That is exactly what happens to us when we are in anguish. We do not realize that Jesus is in our boat—everything is going to be fine.

<u>3) Third thing that happens is that we forget all the good things God has done for us.</u> We previously saw how when the people of Israel were anguished, they demanded things of God. They began to renege on God, saying He brought them out of Egypt to die in the desert. Although we might judge the people of Israel when we read of their attitude, we also do the same when we fall into similar situations. The enemy takes advantage of these circumstances to keep us from remembering what God has done in our lives and how far He has brought us. The psalmist David constantly praised God and recalled His great wonders. In Psalm 103, David confronted his soul and demanded that it bless God and not forget his benefits. To forget the things God has done in our lives weakens our faith and invites doubt into our heart. When there are fights and disagreements in our relationships, we bring to light all the bad things that the person has done. All the good things the person has done are put aside as if they

had little to no value. Perhaps the good things far outweigh the bad, but anguish blinds the person to remember only the bad parts of the relationship. This is exactly what we do with the Lord when we are in the midst of negative circumstances in life. We begin to blame God for the bad things, even going to great lengths to disrespect God. We should visit Calvary's cross repeatedly to keep His sacrifice fresh in our minds and to remember not only everything God did for us but also what He is doing and that which He will do—if we allow Him. When doubt tries to enter our minds, we must hold fast to the incomparable experience that one day turned us from the way of death and eternal condemnation to the path that leads us to the heavenly city and to eternal life. None of us can say that we have not gone through anxieties. But there is a big difference in experiencing moments of anguish and adversity and being dominated by a spirit of anguish. Both feelings are product of life's trials, and the adverse situations that come into our lives, but it is up to us not to let ourselves be controlled by anguish. In 1 Corinthians 6:12, the Apostle Paul says, "All things are lawful unto me, but all things are not expedient: all things are lawful for me, but I will not be brought under the power of any." Some people say that they cannot control their feelings of anguish, because it is much stronger than they are. I tend to differ with that idea, because 2 Timothy 1:7 says: "For God hath not given us the spirit of fear; but of power, and of love, and of a sound mind." We have in our hands powerful weapons that God has given us. When we activate these truths in our life, in our family,

What Happens When I allow the Spirit of Anguish to control me?

and in our situations, God will be glorified. 2 Peter 1:5-10 says: "And beside this, giving all diligence, add to your faith virtue; and to virtue knowledge; and to knowledge temperance; and to temperance patience; and to patience godliness; and to godliness brotherly kindness; and to brotherly kindness charity. For if these things be in you, and abound, they make you that ye shall neither be barren nor unfruitful in the knowledge of our Lord Jesus Christ. But he that lacks these things is blind, and cannot see afar off, and hath forgotten that he was purged from his old sins. Wherefore the rather, brethren, give diligence to make your calling and election sure: for if ye do these things, ye shall never fall."

The Apostle Paul in 1Timothy 1:12-14 says: "And I thank Christ Jesus our Lord, who hath enabled me, for that he counted me faithful, putting me into the ministry; who was before a blasphemer, and a persecutor, and injurious: but I obtained mercy, because I did it ignorantly in unbelief. And the grace of our Lord was exceeding abundant with faith and love which is in Christ Jesus." It may be that until today you have committed many errors because of ignorance and that as a result of these errors, you may find yourself in anguish. The law of sowing and reap is very real, but God is a God of opportunities. The Word of God is faithful and true and it says that seven times will the just fall but God will lift him up. He makes all things new. You can't allow the spirit of anguish to dominate you to the point that you stop walking with God. You are an important instrument in the hands of God. You have a mission to fulfill in this land.

If you fall in a hollow litany, you will be numb and fail to discover and fulfill God's purpose for your life. Many souls need to hear you talk about how the Most High God saved your life and the wonders He has done for you. Romans Chapter 10:14 reads " ...and how shall they believe in him of whom they have not heard? And how shall they hear without a preacher? "

Every person that falls under a spirit of anguish experiences negative feelings toward themselves because they have very low self-esteem. The enemy is responsible for making you feel worthless, that you will never accomplish anything, that you are wasting your time in the church, and that God already gave up on you and he will never use you for anything. You feel rejected by church people and by God himself. Please note that Satan achieves his destructive goals by prompting you to declare the negative thoughts that make you feel inferior. When this happens, we never use second or third person. We speak these negatives about ourselves. For example, we begin to declare things like: "I am a failure or "I am no good." Maybe when we look in the mirror, we say, "I am ugly" or "I am fat." Sometimes we declare: "I know I will not achieve my goals or my dreams." These expressions are not what we want for our lives. Once Satan manages to make us express these derogatory things regarding ourselves, the doors are wide open for the spirit of anguish to continue its destructive work. Satan does not know our thoughts. The Devil throws darts at our mind hoping to see if any of them hits home. With these tricks, he causes Christians to slowly drift away

What Happens When I allow the Spirit of Anguish to control me?

from the congregation and violate the boundaries God has set for us. When we are totally on our own, we are outside of His divine protection and give Satan the opportunity to control our minds and destroy our spiritual temple.

It does not stop there. Although at first glance, things may appear normal, strongholds begin to form as the person conforms to the things of this world. Sin no longer exists for them. These forces undermine their spiritual temple; now everything is for the sake of appearance— they have no essence of God. That is why the Apostle Paul speaking to Timothy says to him in his first epistle chapter 4:1-3, "Now the Spirit speaks expressly, that in the latter times some shall depart from the faith, giving heed to seducing spirits, and doctrines of devils; Speaking lies in hypocrisy; having their conscience seared with a hot iron; Forbidding to marry, and commanding to abstain from meats, which God hath created to be received with thanksgiving of them which believe and know the truth." In other words, everything that they preached and identified as unpleasant to God now they begin to deny or to accept it and pass it off as acceptable. Their moral compass deteriorates rapidly and they are not convicted of sin, because they have grieved the Holy Spirit within them. There is great danger in this because the Bible says: "Woe to him that calls good evil and evil good."

I saw a woman tormented by the spirit of anguish recently at the time that my precious mother went to be with the Lord. It was a person who was not part of the family, but a family friend. She had been warned that my mother was in her last hours and hastened to get together with us children and other family members. From the moment she entered into the bedroom where the body of my mother was, she began to tremble intensely. Her anguish was such that she would not hear words of consolation and had to leave. Then she wanted to make sure she went to the wake; once there, she cried intensely. When I saw an opportunity to comfort her, I encouraged her to look at the nine children, grandchildren, nephews and great-grandchildren who were quietly comforted because we were absolutely convinced that my mother was in a better place with the Lord. Between cries and sobs, she told me she remembered her grandmother, who also had been a Godly woman. She also shared with me that she felt much resentment against God for having taken her grandmother and that she did not have the opportunity to apologize for the bad things she had done to her. It was not until that moment that I realized she was being tormented by a spirit of anguish. Any words I could speak to her at that moment would not heal her hurting heart. This person maintained an open file that should have been saved in the permanent memory of her mind many years before. Unfortunately, she did not have the slightest interest in allowing God to enter into her life and to allow Him to set her free from her anguish. When we give in to this feeling, we become puppets of the spirit of anguish. Whenever the opportunity presents itself, our anguish will manifest itself. Until then, we remain blinded to the reality that lies ahead.

It's Time to Change

I would like to share something I heard recently and I found it very true: "Change your way of thinking and this will change the way you live." Everything that exists in this world is exposed to change. From birth until the day we die, our body is trained and designed to experience changes in our physiognomy. Some people want to stop or delay these changes using creams, exercises, operations and many other things. However, they are only delaying these changes that are, frankly, inevitable. Within all of nature, human beings are the only ones who resist the changes God designed for us. Once in our comfort zones, we don't want to leave. When we are accustomed to a pattern or a daily routine, it is very difficult to change. The changes that we go through in our lives many times tend to be painful. Other times a change that seems to be painful in the beginning can have positive results. When we are reluctant to accept a change that we know is inevitable, the pain is even more intense. It is possible that we fear a change because we are unfamiliar with what lies on the other side or how the change will affect us. Resistance is normal in times of change, but there is nothing more beautiful than surrendering in the presence of the Lord and giving

DELIVER ME FROM MY ANGUISH, LORD!

him all our struggles. When we let go of those things that are holding back our spiritual growth, God begins to glorify himself in our lives. In Him we will find the strength that we need to be free of anguish and discouragement. (Phil. 4:13) I can do all things through Christ who strengthens me.

God wants us to seek his presence and to give him every aspect of our life. When we speak of the spirit of anguish, the person has to be willing to go through a series of changes. Some think that the people that surround them are the ones who need to change. Some time ago, I heard a brother in Christ talk about his family; he told us he had a continuing struggle regarding family matters but that his wife and children had to change. When he prayed, he asked God to change them because he could not continue this struggle. One day, while he prayed, God revealed to him that he was the one who had to change and not his wife and children. Since that day, he began to change certain things in his life. With time, he realized that because of his new attitude, all family members were receptive to changing, though they did not realize it.

It is said that if you want to get different results, you need to change or alter the way you do things. Over the course of my life, I have experienced countless changes. Changes in my body, changes in my family, work changes, changes in the church, changes in my way of thinking toward many things, changes in eating habits, changes in regard to my friends, changes in physical appearance. In fact, my entire life has been full of constant change. Many of the changes have been very painful for me. Some changes have come about naturally, while others have been provoked by me or by other people. Not all changes in my life have had good results, but others have. There have been times when I thought I could not triumph over changes, but through all my experiences, today I can say without a shadow of a doubt that I have seen the hand of God with me, guiding me, holding me, caring for me, supporting me, comforting me and—best of all—loving me. Glory to God for his love and mercy that have always been with me—even when it seemed like I was all alone!

How can I be free?

I have always been attracted to the story of David and Goliath. Allegorically, we have always compared David with Christian men and women when they face Goliaths—or adversity—in their lives. There are ten steps that will help you to defeat those giants that come into your life:

1. <u>The First Step</u> is to recognize the cause. In 1 Samuel 17:25, David had a reason for fighting Goliath. This reason motivated him to fight. He could see with spiritual eyes and visualize the victory first hand. David could not endure seeing this evil man defy the people of Israel any longer. The challenge? Any Israelite who fought against the giant and won would require the Philistines to serve the men of Israel. Conversely, if the giant conquered the people of Israel, then, the people of God would serve the Philistines. The person who is in midst of a spiritual struggle and is tormented by a spirit of anguish must do a self-evaluation and study their present situation. Identify where you are, and decide where you want to be or what you want to accomplish. You must first determine what is the root of the problem that is causing you so much distress. Identify the source. Calculate your risk and the expected results when you come against the giant

that is defying you. I think that this was precisely what the Psalmist in Psalm 42, verse 5 expressed, when he asked his soul: "Why art thou cast down, O my soul? And why art thou disquieted in me? Hope thou in God: for I shall yet praise him for the help of his countenance." In this Psalm, David was very sad—he thought God had forgotten him. In verse 9, he said: "I will say unto God my rock, why hast thou forgotten me? Why go I mourning because of the oppression of the enemy?" David tried to find the root of the spirit of anguish that had seized him. It is of great importance that you examine your situation. Ask yourself if this situation or problem is part of your past or your present and how it can affect your future. Then ask yourself if it has a solution. If your answer is no, then release it immediately and leave it in your past because it is already too late to change it. If your answer is yes, then proceed to the second step.

2. <u>The Second Step</u> is to reject the negativism and make a firm decision. Let us remember that David was a shepherd—not a giant slayer (1Samuel 17:21-30). His brothers tried to discourage him because they saw him as a small, defenseless kid. We have to be determined to be free from anguish—it has to come from within you. No one else can do it for you. As humans, we spend our entire life making decisions. This behavior begins from the moment we are born. However, many times we do not make the right decisions at the right time. When we listen to the voices of those who do not have the same vision we do, this will often prevent us from being free of things that bind us and cause us great distress. We fall into

an emotional labyrinth with no apparent way out. Nehemiah was a man who was passionate about the things of God. While he was cupbearer in the king's house, Nehemiah learned that Jerusalem had been struck by its enemies, that the wall had been knocked down, and the doors of the city had been burned down. From the moment that the young man learned about this situation he began to pray and fast. Then with approval of the King, he left to restore Jerusalem. As soon as the work was organized and he recruited people for the work, the opposition began. First it arose in the form of mockery (Nehemiah 2:19-20), but Nehemiah overcame with confidence in God. This was followed by anger and contempt, which he defeated with prayer and hard work (Chapter 4:4-6). Then, conspiracy, which was defeated by watchfulness and prayer. Constant love triumphed over discouragement (Chapter 4:10-14), and self-denial defeated selfish greed in Chapter 5:1-17. What a beautiful story! The verse that is most commonly used by ministers when they talk about this story is Nehemiah 6:3. Sanballat and Geshem tried to discourage Nehemiah at all costs. They intended to show that they were interested in the restoration of Israel, pretending to form alliances with Nehemiah, only to make him lose focus on his vision. Nehemiah sent messengers to them: "I am doing a great work, so that I cannot come down: why should the work cease, whilst I leave it, and come down to you?" Four times these men insisted deterring him from the restoration of the city of God, but they did not achieve their goal because Nehemiah trusted that God would give him the victory.

When we begin to listen to the voices of those who do not want to help us move forward, we should send them a similar message: "I am doing great work so I cannot go down to you because the work will cease."

3. The Third Step is: Disclose and declare your intentions against the giant of anguish. David verbalized his faith by declaring that his God would give him the victory. Begin to trust in God. James 4:8 says: "Draw close to God, and he will draw close to you." Hebrews 4:16 says, "Let us therefore come boldly unto the throne of grace that we may obtain mercy and find grace to help in time of need." Some of us find it very difficult to let go of our burdens. Because of David's close relationship with God, he was sure that as he defeated the lion and the bear, he could also get the victory over Goliath. David recognized that he overcame not with his power but with the power of God. If we seek to maintain a relationship with God as David did, we can also declare war on the enemy because we know that greater is he that is within us than the one who is the world.

It is important to know how to cry out to God in the midst of anguish. Sadly, many times when we are distressed, the last thing we do is cry out to God. I have heard people say that God is too busy for them to bother Him with their problems. What they don't know is that God is concerned about each detail of your life. He is attentive to the cries of his children. Psalms 34:17: "The righteous cry and the LORD hears them and delivers them out of all their troubles." It is easier to hear and comfort a person who is ill than to have to deal with someone who is in distress and striving alone. Proverbs 18:14 reads: "The spirit of a man will sustain his infirmity; but a wounded spirit who can bear?" When we have something in which we need God to intervene, we must freely and persistently cry out until we obtain that which we need from God. 1 Peter 2:2-3 urges: "As newborn babes, desire the sincere milk of the word that ye may grow thereby: If so be ye have tasted that the Lord is gracious." When a newborn is hungry, he or she will not stop crying until they are fed. This is a great example of how we should persistently approach God when it comes to getting our prayers answered.

As I mentioned earlier, many of the Biblical men and women of God were fraught with anguish, some of them on more than one occasion; but they knew that if they cried out to God, He would answer their prayers and free them from their anguish. Jeremiah 33:3 says: "Call unto me, and I will answer thee, and show thee great and mighty things, which thou know not." When we cry out to God, we have gone beyond a simple prayer and we raise our voice to God with certainty that He is powerful to undo any bondage we might be facing. Psalms 34:6 says: "This poor man cried, and the LORD heard him, and saved him out of all his troubles." It is sad to say, but what many people do in the midst of trials is move away from God. Others seek consolation and advice in other persons who are not spiritually trained to advise them and fall into a worse situation. The first thing we must do is

How can I be free?

to direct our cry toward heaven. In Psalm 55:2-3 the Psalmist says: "Attend unto me, and hear me: I mourn in my complaint, and make a noise; Because of the voice of the enemy, because of the oppression of the wicked: for they cast iniquity upon me, and in wrath they hate me." Notice that he wanted to be sure that God was attentive to his cry. In verse 16, after having presented his case, he feels sure that all that he has to do is cry out to God. He begins to trust that God is aware of everything that is going on, so he dares to advise others to cast their burdens on the Lord (verse 22). Isaiah 65:14 says: "Behold, my servants shall sing for joy of heart, but ye shall cry for sorrow of heart, and shall howl for vexation of spirit."

4. <u>Fourth Step:</u> Remember your victories of the past. Recall how God brought you from this or that situation with great success. But don't dwell on the past. With the same confidence and trust, walk forward without looking back. Sometimes at the time of our battle, we remember only the fight and not our victory. It is important that we know and remember from where God brought us with His strong arm. Let us exercise selective memory and relive those moments. Let us remember the people of Israel when it was time to move out of Egypt. There is a time to cry out to God and a time to move forward. In Exodus 14:15, Moses cries out to God, "And the LORD said unto Moses, Wherefore cries thou unto me? Speak unto the children of Israel, that they go forward." He said it was not time to cry; it was time to move on. Moses remembered how God had given

him victory when he needed it most and was confident that he would emerge victorious from this new challenge.

5. <u>Fifth Step:</u> Dress with your own armor. In 1 Samuel 17:38-39, it was impossible for David to use the armor of Saul because it weighed too much. Let us not use the armor of another brother. Let God use you as you are with what you have. You have your own talents and virtues that God has given you. Don't be fooled into imitating other people and how they do things. Be genuine for God and know that he has given you an armor of your own. This has been the point of failure for many people. They think that only certain brothers or sisters can cope with certain situations. They think that because they didn't have some preparation or attend some college in particular, they are not able to fight spiritual battles or to live to their potential are not trained to apply Biblical principles to their spiritual struggles. This severely limits their potential in their Christian walk. There is no specific pattern or method designed for your particular battle. God will properly equip you with what you need to fight your giant.

6. <u>Sixth step</u>: Declare your faith publicly (1 Samuel 17:45-46). Not only do you need to mention your faith, you should sing it, yell it out, walk it out, and declare with a strong voice what God has done in your life. Demonstrate that you know in whom you have believed. Begin to defy those giants in your life and declare your victory by faith. James 5:16 says: "The effectual fervent prayer of a righteous man availed much." At times, we must open our mouths, yet we remain silent. In Psalm 27:3, David declared: "Though a

host should encamp against me, my heart shall not fear: though war should rise against me, in this will I be confident." Psalms 34:7 says: "The angel of the LORD encamped round about them that fear him, and delivers them." Fear is not welcome here. Doing this takes someone bold and courageous who will be used by God.

7. <u>Seventh Step</u>: Run toward the enemy (1 Samuel 17:48): "And David put his hand in his bag, and took thence a stone, and slang it, and smote the Philistine in his forehead, that the stone sunk into his forehead; and he fell upon his face to the earth." The only way to kill the giant is by squaring up to it courageously and aggressively. Attack discouragement with words of hope and with a song of joy. You have to do your part. Run with purpose toward the giant and don't be intimidated by anyone or anything. Do not attempt to escape your problems or the situation that you may be facing. You may feel that you are fighting alone, but God is with you as a mighty giant to give you the victory. Psalms 37:39: "But the salvation of the righteous is of the LORD: he is their strength in the time of trouble." Tremble at the power and anointing of God. The anointing is the essential ingredient to being free from a spirit of anguish (Isaiah 10:27): "and the yoke shall be destroyed because of the anointing." 1 John 2:20 says, "But ye have an unction from the Holy One, and ye know all things." God has not given us the spirit of fear. We need to stand firmly and run with the assurance that God will fight our battle.

8. <u>Eighth Step:</u> Cut off the Head of the giant (1 Samuel 17:51): "Therefore David ran, and stood upon the Philistine, and took his

sword, and drew it out of the sheath thereof, and slew him, and cut off his head therewith. And when the Philistines saw their champion was dead, they fled." It is very important that we cut the head of the giant because by doing so, we evidence that the giant is dead. When you knock the giant down, leave it in the past, pull it from its roots so that it does not re-emerge. Galatians 2:20 reads: "I am crucified with Christ: nevertheless I live; yet not I, but Christ lives in me: and the life which I now live in the flesh I live by the faith of the Son of God, who loved me, and gave himself for me." When we kill the giant that haunts us, the living spirit of Jesus comes to dwell in our lives. We cannot be happy when we are constantly thinking of the past, wishing we could relive the past to change things that did not turn out as we wanted. Those words that were never said, those questions that were left without answers, the places that were not visited, the dreams that never became reality, the explanation that was never given. All these things belong in the past. Today is a new day and another opportunity to begin to write a new story. These memories must be nipped in the bud. Forget them, bury them, burn or remove them as you wish. The memories that have left their marks on our hearts are precisely that—memories. They are not our present and definitely not our future.

The Word of God tells us that we must continue to walk forward. Our Christian path is intended to move forward at all times. It seems that the Bible contradicts itself when in many places it commands us not to let us remember things past, as in Ecclesiastes 7:10: "Say not thou, what is the cause that the former days were better than these? For thou dost not enquire wisely concerning this." While in other passages, we are encouraged to remember things past. In reality, when we recall the things of yesterday, almost always what is remembered are the bad things or things that caused us harm. Recall the story of Lot's wife: She became a pillar of salt by looking at the things that were lagging behind in Sodom and Gomorrah. God had given them strict instructions that they were to leave running and not look at what they left behind. It is possible that she was attached to material things, or maybe her curiosity caused her to look back. Regardless, the results were deadly. Paul knew that the things he left behind did not compare to what he had received from God. This is why he said in Philippians 3:13-14: "Brethren, I count not myself to have apprehended: but this one thing I do, forgetting those things which are behind, and reaching forth unto those things which are before, I press toward the mark for the prize of the high calling of God in Christ Jesus."

9. <u>Ninth Step:</u> Rejoice in the Lord (1 Samuel 17:52). "And the men of Israel and of Judah arose, and shouted, and pursued the Philistines, until thou come to the valley, and to the gates of Ekron. And the wounded of the Philistines fell down by the way to Shaaraim, even unto Gath, and unto Ekron." When you have obtained the victory, give glory to God. The book of Proverbs tells us: "Trust in the Lord with all your heart and lean not unto thine own understanding." God has promised to always be with those who

trust in Him, especially with those who recognize that without Him, there's nothing we can do. It is He who gives us strength when we have none, this is why we sing: "Let the weak man say I am strong." It is good to rejoice when you have the victory, but remember: You have to be ready for the next battle against the next giant that rises up against you. "Cry out and shout, thou inhabitant of Zion: for great is the Holy One of Israel in the midst of thee." Like David danced before the ark, take time to rejoice in presence of the Lord. Psalms 138:4-7 says, "All the kings of the earth shall praise thee, O LORD, when they hear the words of thy mouth. Yea, they shall sing in the ways of the LORD: for great is the glory of the LORD. Though the LORD be high, yet hath he respect unto the lowly: but the proud he knoweth afar off. Though I walk in the midst of trouble, thou wilt revive me: thou shalt stretch forth thine hand against the wrath of mine enemies, and thy right hand shall save me."

10. <u>Tenth Step</u>: Review and enjoy the rewards (1 Samuel 17:53-54). "And the children of Israel returned from chasing after the Philistines, and they spoiled their tents. And David took the head of the Philistine, and brought it to Jerusalem; but he put his armor in his tent." After having overcome the giant, don't forget to collect your reward. In the book of Revelation, we find a series of promises for he who overcomes. Let's review these:

Revelation 2:7: "He that hath an ear, let him hear what the Spirit saith unto the churches; to him that overcomes will I give to eat of the tree of life, which is in the midst of the paradise of God."

How can I be free?

Revelation 2:11 "He that hath an ear, let him hear what the Spirit saith unto the churches; He that overcomes shall not be hurt of the second death."

Revelation 2:17 "He that hath an ear, let him hear what the Spirit saith unto the churches; To him that overcomes will I give to eat of the hidden manna, and will give him a white stone, and in the stone a new name written, which no man knows saving he that receives it."

Revelation 2:26-27 "And he that overcomes, and kept my works unto the end, to him will I give power over the nations: And he shall rule them with a rod of iron; as the vessels of a potter shall they be broken to shivers: even as I received of my Father."

Revelation 3:5 "He that overcomes, the same shall be clothed in white raiment; and I will not blot out his name out of the book of life, but I will confess his name before my Father, and before his angels."

Revelation 3:12 "Him that overcomes will I make a pillar in the temple of my God, and he shall go no more out: and I will write upon him the name of my God, and the name of the city of my God, which is new Jerusalem, which cometh down out of heaven from my God: and I will write upon him my new name."

Revelation 3:21: "To him that overcomes will I grant to sit with me in my throne, even as I also overcame, and am set down with my Father in his throne."

Revelation 21:7 "He that overcomes shall inherit all things; and I will be his God, and he shall be my son."

All these promises should motivate you as a Christian to press on. Trials, tribulations and even anguish may attempt to bring you down, but when you look at the Scriptures and take ownership of these promises, you will have the strength to carry on.

God Has Everything Under Control

When I was about two years old, my mother was admitted to a hospital for people with tuberculosis. The doctors discovered that her lungs were completely destroyed because of this terrible disease. According to the medical community, she would remain in that place until she died; there was no hope for her. I was the third and youngest of her children at the time. The doctors told her that she could no longer have more children because her health would not allow it. I can only imagine the pain my mother felt—she was barely 24 years of age at the time. To think that she would no longer see her three children and her husband caused great sadness. Although there were many questions without answers and so much pain in her soul, she was able to recall that a few months earlier, had surrendered her heart to Jesus Christ and made him Lord of her life. I imagine that, being a new Christian, she would be prone to weakened faith and even reneging on God. Although a spirit of anguish threatened to torment her, she hung on to the experience she had with the Great Physician.

It was then when she exercised her mustard-seed faith and began to declare the things that were not as if they were. Taking the Bible in her hands and crying out to God, she asked him to talk to her through his Word. At that moment, she opened her Bible, and God took her directly to the book of Exodus chapter 15, verse 26, a promise of God: "And said, If thou wilt diligently hearken to the voice of the LORD thy God, and wilt do that which is right in his sight, and wilt give ear to his commandments, and keep all his statutes, I will put none of these diseases upon thee, which I have brought upon the Egyptians: for I am the LORD that healeth thee." What a powerful promise! God was telling her "I am the Lord your healer." That was a great revelation in and of itself, but there was a condition that needed to be met in order to obtain the promise. The beginning of the verse says: "If thou shalt hearken diligently the voice of the Lord your God and do what is right in front of his eyes and wilt give ear to his commandments, and keep all his statutes." When she read these words, her life was impacted in a powerful way. These words gave her courage to put her faith into action. As time went by, God taught her to have patience and to wait on His time. Two years later, God glorified himself and healed her body. She was able to leave the hospital totally healthy. The doctors could not explain why her lungs, which had been totally destroyed at one time, were now as good as new. During her stay in the hospital, she was able to organize a group of Christians who met regularly to worship God. God gave her this opportunity to witness healings and to lead other patients to salvation. Even in the midst of her anguish, she knew that as a child of God, there was a purpose for her being there.

God Has Everything Under Control

My mother was a woman of God with a spotless testimony. She knew the Word very well and always sought refuge in its pages for divine consolation. However, this did not release her from human feelings such as anguish. While she was in the hospital, they cleared her to go home for a few days. While at home, she became pregnant. Once she gave birth to her fourth child, Juan Marcos, he was taken away from her hands and handed to my father. At that time, my father had begun to work in the missionary field as a pastor and it was practically impossible for him to raise a newborn baby, so they agreed to let an elderly couple of the church take charge of the child. When my mother left the hospital, she sought the return of her son, but could not recover him. The couple who had him all that time bonded with him and refused to return him to my mother. Being the woman of God that she was, she decided to leave it in the hands of the Lord. Not having her child alongside her with her other children caused my mother ongoing sadness and distress, but she waited on the Lord. She knew that in some way, God would ensure that her child would return home. I remember that twelve years had gone by and the only time we saw my brother Marcos was when they would casually allow him to come visit us. Since that time, my mother had other children (we are nine in total). On a specific New Year's Eve, as we closed out the year, God used a brother in the church to call people to the altar to bring in the New Year in church-wide prayer. He challenged every person who had an unanswered prayer request to leave it on the altar that night, trusting that God was going to reply in the New Year. That night my mother literally threw herself on the concrete altar. She cried out in the Lord's presence because she wanted to have her child with her without having to seek legal assistance. When she arose from the altar, she told us that she was no longer going to weep about it because God was going to handle it. A little past noon on New Year's Day, we saw a child coming toward our house riding a bicycle. It was my brother Marcos. Something had happened at his foster parent's home, and they were ready to give him back to my parents voluntarily. This was one of the many times that God was glorified in our family. You don't need to fight with your physical strength. When you surrender to him, God will stir things up in such a way that they work out for your good.

There is another incident that I want to share about my mother. When we were still children, she endured a very difficult situation that left a very bitter feeling within her for many years. At first sight, it seemed that over the years, the situation had been forgotten and that everything in her life was progressing perfectly well. After all, she was a leader in the church and the sounding board for her family. As an adult, I came home for a visit with her, and I came across a surprise. I noticed something different in her face. Even her smile was more relaxed. She told me that God delivered her from the anguish she had been carrying for many years. She confessed to me that she cried herself to sleep night after night because of the pain in her soul. Although she prayed and served the Lord faithfully, she had not allowed God to work in this area of her life. That day, tired of feeling this way, she cried to the Lord, so that he would take away the pain in her chest. While she prayed and poured out her soul before the Lord, God began to heal her wounds. When she got up from her knees, she began to look at things differently. God broke the spirit of anguish, bringing back the joy of salvation into her heart. For the first time after so many years, she felt a desire in her heart to forgive the people who had done so much harm to her many years back.

As a Christian, you must strive toward spiritual maturity. Giving up your pain and anguish to God and allowing him to heal the wounds of your heart requires great spiritual maturity. As believers, we must seek to grow in the grace of God. We cannot stay in the first stage— when we first met the Lord. God expects and demands maturity so we can have power and be used for his glory. The Christian who does not mature spiritually is a person who is spiritually abnormal. 1 Corinthians 13:11 reads: "When I was a child, I spake as a child, I understood as a child, I thought as a child: but when I became a man, I put away childish things." 1 Corinthians 14:20 urges us: "Brethren, be not children in understanding: howbeit in malice be ye children, but in understanding be men." It is a daily process of growth. Ephesians 4:13 says, "Till we all come in the unity of the faith, and of the knowledge of the Son of God, unto a perfect man, unto the measure of the stature of the fulness of Christ." Also Proverbs 4:18 says: "But the path of the just is as the shining light, that shineth more and more unto the perfect day." All of these Biblical passages point out the importance of spiritual growth.

Growing in the truths of the Word of God is how we can reach that maturity needed to rid ourselves of the burden that assails us. Hebrews 5:14 says, "But strong meat belongs to them that are of full age, even those who by reason of use have their senses exercised to discern both good and evil." As we increase in maturity, we begin to see things differently. I love the way the Psalmist expresses himself in Psalm 119:67: "Before I was afflicted I went astray: but now have I kept thy word." Suppose you have a child who is 17 years of age and does not want to learn how to drive because he wants to rely on you for transportation all the time. This is not normal. At this age, the young person typically longs for independence and wants to get to places on his or her own. That's exactly what happens with us; many times we want God to take us everywhere. We don't want to strive even when it is time to walk on our own. We want God do that which is humanly possible, when that is what we must do. We can hold God responsible for the impossible, but we are responsible for the things we can do. When we take control of that which is within our control, we begin to move forward in faith trusting and walking in his promises.

A story in the Bible shows us how we can fall into great anguish because of disobedience. I'm talking about the story of Jonah. This man had been sent by God to preach to Nineveh, a big city, which would be destroyed by God if they did not repent. Jonah did not want to obey God and took a ship that was going in a totally opposite direction. While he was on the ship sleeping, there arose a great storm in the middle of the sea. The captain of the ship woke Jonah, and they told him to cry to his God for mercy so they would not perish. All those who were on the ship were distressed. Jonah recognized that it was the hand of God causing the big storm, so he told the crew to throw him overboard. God sent a large fish to bring him to where God wanted him to go in the first place. Doesn't that sound to you like what some of us do when God sends us to do something and we go into the opposite direction? When things just don't seem to go right, we end up in anguish asking God why.

What is so interesting about this story is that Jonah was distressed and in the belly of a large fish. Faced with the dilemma of what to do, he decided to cry out to God. God in his mercy allowed the fish to return to the Nineveh seashore. Many times in the midst of our anguish, we feel trapped in a tunnel of depression, as was Jonah within that great fish. The Psalmist says in Psalms 130:1-2: "Out of the depths have I cried unto thee, O LORD. Lord, hear my voice: let thine ears be attentive to the voice of my supplications." This is what happens when God sets some plans in motion in our lives. When he begins to work on some of our issues, we know we are being equipped for the time when He will use us. When our finite minds cannot understand what God is doing with us behind the scenes, we get discouraged and lose focus of the vision and of what is really happening.

When this happens, we tend to make hasty decisions that are not in agreement with what God wants for our life. In the long run, we bring unfortunate consequences on ourselves and, in many cases, spiritual ruin. Every time we disobey the voice of God, we are simply delaying his plan and his purpose in our lives. It is difficult to be led by God when we do not walk in the spirit. The flesh and the spirit have a constant struggle. The Word ensures that the desires of the flesh are contrary to those of God. On the other hand, when we give ourselves to the Lord and we refuse to please the desires of the flesh, God begins to do great things with us and uses us to help others who might be experiencing similar situations. God has great blessings for us.

The story of Jonah also shows us that when our anguish leads us to make hasty decisions, we affect ourselves and those all those around us. If we make wise decisions, those that are pleasing to God, we will obtain great blessings for ourselves and for our loved ones. On the other hand, if we choose to walk in disobedience, we will carry God's punishment and bring ruin to ourselves and our loved ones. In recent years, there has been a television commercial about depression. As the voice in the commercial asks who is affected by depression, the images show photos of family members and even pets. This is reality. When we are depressed or tormented by a spirit of anguish, everything in our environment is affected. We become incapable of fulfilling our different roles, whether as a parent, or as children, friends, husbands, or wives. We become unproductive individuals in society.

When we are overwhelmed by anguish, we cannot operate at full capacity because our life and all our senses revolve around self-pity—we are unable to think of anything other than ourselves. The language of tears will move the heart of God because God doesn't reject a humble and contrite heart. Isaiah 65:24 has a powerful promise God that you can recite when you feel like you are falling into anguish: "And it shall come to pass, that before they call, I will answer; and while they are yet speaking, I will hear."

The great advantage that Christians have over non-Christians is that we have the assurance from God that once we cry out, God is listening. 1 John 4:4 reads: "Ye are of God, little children, and have overcome them: because greater is he that is in you, than he that is in the world." The apostle Paul addresses the Corinthians in 2 Corinthians 4:8-9 saying: "We are troubled on every side, yet not distressed; we are perplexed, but not in despair; Persecuted, but not forsaken; cast down, but not destroyed." Later in verses 16-18, we read: "For which cause we faint not; but though our outward man perish, yet the inward man is renewed day by day. For our light affliction, which is but for a moment, worketh for us a far more exceeding and eternal weight of glory; While we look not at the things which are seen, but at the things which are not seen: for the things which are seen are temporal; but the things which are not seen are eternal." One of the things I like about the Pauline Epistles is the transformation of Saul. Despite the fact that he had received a direct call on his life by God, he was not exempt from trials and tribulations. Even more, God sent Ananias to tell Saul that he was going to use him as a vessel to bring the message to the Gentiles, to kings, and to the children of Israel, but that God would also show him the great things he must suffer for His name's sake (Acts 9:16). Therefore, Paul knew in advance that it was not going to be easy to serve the Lord. Of one thing he was certain, and that was that the One who called him would remove all of his anxiety. Suppose that Paul, upon reaching Lystra, where he would be stoned, determined that he was no longer going to preach the gospel because he could not continue to suffer persecution and suffering. Or suppose he confined himself to a small room and spent his time complaining about what had happened to him in Lystra. We would not have these beautiful Epistles which he was inspired to write by the Holy Spirit today.

When you think of your past and everything that you have gone through, remember that everything happens for a purpose. You did not come into this world by chance or coincidence. If you love the Lord, Romans 8:28 is a great comfort: "And we know that all things work together for good to them that love God, to them who are the called according to his purpose." The Apostle makes it clear that everything that happens to us—whether positive or negative—will result in our benefit. Anyone who loves God and is called according to His purpose can believe that God has a perfect plan for their life. In God, there are no coincidences.

Paul stated clearly that we cannot allow anything—including anguish—to detach us from the love of God. In Romans 8:35, he said: "Who shall separate us from the love of Christ? Shall tribulation, or distress, or persecution, or famine, or nakedness, or peril, or sword?" In this chapter, the Apostle wants to remind us that we may have many things that will possibly attempt to disconnect us from the love of God. He knew this because he himself had to go through all these things. This was not a coincidence. Everything was within God's plans.

This chapter of Romans thrills me, and I can almost imagine myself listening to the Apostle speak in verses 37 to 39: "Nay, in all these things we are more than conquerors through him that loved us. For I am persuaded, that neither death, nor life, nor angels, nor principalities, nor powers, nor things present, nor things to come, Nor height, nor depth, nor any other creature, shall be able to separate us from the love of God, which is in Christ Jesus our Lord." What a powerful declaration of faith! This expression comes from a grateful heart for the work God brought about in him. What about you? Are you grateful for God? 1 Peter 1:22-23 says, "Seeing ye have purified your souls in obeying the truth through the Spirit unto unfeigned love of the brethren, see that ye love one another with a pure heart fervently: Being born again, not of corruptible seed, but of incorruptible, by the word of God, which liveth and abideth for ever." We must renew our minds every day and not let memories of the past deprive us of the happiness that Christ offers. Ephesians 4:23 reads: "And be renewed in the spirit of your mind."

I venture to assert that, when my mother was in the hospital, she did not think that God had future plans for her life. In fact, with so little knowledge of the Word of God, the last thing she expected was that He would use her as the vessel to restore worship to the one and only God in that place. One of the things she told us was that she met two ladies and became close friends with them there. One of them was named Iluminada and they called her "Lumi", the other one was Paquita. These two young women were also ill with tuberculosis in their lungs. They had come to that place before my mother, but they had no intention of seeking God. Even more, they rebelled and blamed God for their illness. But God wanted to use my mother so that they would be reconciled with the Lord. She met them at their bedside each night and asked them to join her in prayer. Together, they began to search for God.

She testified that when the lights went off in the hospital each night, the three women would head to the bathroom, where they had cleaned off a quiet corner to pray to their God while other patients slept. This was the secret to their greatest victories while in the hospital. Every day, they saw patients die from this terrible disease. Lumi had been in that place for a long time and she had undergone several surgeries. Doctors said her body could not withstand any other surgeries. Even more, if the wound in her womb was to open up again, she would surely die. Nevertheless, God had spoken a word of healing to her while they were praying in their secret place. He promised total healing and assured them that Lumi was not only going to leave that place but also preach his Word throughout the world. One morning, while my mother was in her bed, with her breakfast in hand ready to start eating, teammates came running with the news that Lumi was bleeding from her wound. At that time, my mother cried out to God and asked: "How is this possible, Lord?" At that very moment, she heard the voice of God audibly, as a gentle breeze whisper to her ear: "So my name may be glorified!" She immediately dropped the breakfast tray and ran to the bed where Lumi's body lay. Making her way through the patients, doctors, and nurses, she came to Lumi. She sat on her bedside, took Lumi's hands between hers, and asked her, "Lumi, in whom have you believed?" Then she began to recite the 23rd Psalm, asking Lumi to recite it with her. Minutes seemed to last forever. As she was finishing the Psalm, she recited the phrase, "Although I walk through the valley of the shadow of death, I will fear no evil, because you are with me." My mother saw Lumi's lips move as she herself repeated the words of the Psalm. Soon after, she opened her eyes and smiled at everyone there. Lumi said, "I felt that as if I was going into a very long tunnel. I saw a bright light at the end. Then, I heard the voice of Ana Elsie (my mother) call me and tell me to come back, so I had to return." Then she went on to say: "I also felt as if a great hand reached into my abdomen and closed a running faucet." God had done an instantaneous miracle right before everyone's eyes. Not only had she come back from death; God instantly closed her wound. Shortly after this, Lumi left that place and was able to travel to many countries of the world preaching the Word and sharing her testimony with many people.

Many times, God leads us through situations that at first sight seem to be quite negative, but God has a purpose with each thing and each situation that comes into our lives. Isaiah 42:6-7 says: "I the LORD have called thee in righteousness, and will hold thine hand, and will keep thee, and give thee for a covenant of the people, for a light of the Gentiles; To open the blind eyes, to bring out the prisoners from the prison, and them that sit in darkness out of the prison house."

Where do you start?

We learn from the Word of God that there is power in prayer. The Christian who does not pray will live in spiritual defeat. Prayer is simply the means by which we communicate with God. Sadly, there are Christians who are intimidated by prayer because they have not learned how beautiful it is to go before the presence of God and feel His tender touch. The Bible recommends that we pray without ceasing. There is no mystery to prayer. It is as simple as opening our lips and expressing to God the things that are in our heart. You do not necessarily have to be on your knees or in a specific position to pray to God. We can do so while we walk, while driving, running, and even working. What matters is that we talk with God; it is not the position in which we do so, nor the place. Prayer should be a daily practice, it is as important as eating, drinking, or sleeping. It is our constant and daily communication with God and keeps us connected to heaven.

God also likes us to worship and praise him. Psalms 22:3 says: "But thou art holy, O thou that inhabitest the praises of Israel." Praise is a very essential tool in the life of every believer. Praise brings deliverance. At the beginning of this book, I said that one of the things that happens to us when we are overwhelmed with a spirit of anguish is that we do not want to praise God. We completely lose the desire to honor God because we are so anxious and drowning in our shame that the enemy does not allow us to worship and praise God. Throughout the Bible, all the victories won by the people of God included praise. Psalm 50:14-15 expresses this very clear: "Offer unto God thanksgiving; and pay thy vows unto the most High: And call upon me in the day of trouble: I will deliver thee, and thou shalt glorify me." What beautiful words of encouragement to praise and worship God! It is very important that we practice this in our daily living.

The Bible tells us about a man whose life was transformed by prayer. This time, I am referring to Jacob. His name means supplanter or impostor because he used deception to obtain the birthright in exchange for a bowl of stew. Although everything was delineated within the divine plan of God, Jacob endured much affliction. No other character in the Bible represents more clearly the conflicts between life's highs and lows than Jacob. If we were to study his life in detail, we would see that he had to face many lows. Sometimes he would reach great heights but again would slide into all sorts of sordid struggles. In the end, he emerged triumphant, despite all his weaknesses. He was an instrument chosen by God. In the course of his life, we see two key truths: (1) The unhappiness produced by his family problems, and (2) The transforming power of communion with God. If we were to diagram his spiritual life, we would see God's divine hand manifested throughout Jacob's human life. In chapter 32 of Genesis, we

Where do you start?

find Jacob distressed at the close proximity of his estranged brother, so he resorted to prayer. Soon thereafter, he spent a full night wrestling with God in a plea of desperation. He obtained the victory, and his name was changed to Israel. Later, he had an affectionate encounter with his brother Esau. Almost immediately, he experienced another low at the disgrace of his daughter Dina and her brothers' vengeance on her abusers. Again, he is in anguish. When he comes to Bethel, he is reminded of his vision and builds an altar to God. In Genesis chapter 35 verses 2-3: "Then Jacob said unto his household, and to all that were with him, Put away the strange gods that are among you, and be clean, and change your garments: And let us arise, and go up to Bethel; and I will make there an altar unto God, who answered me in the day of my distress, and was with me in the way which I went." This was a remarkable event in Jacob's life. First, he ensured he was prepared to worship. This is very important. We need to obey and get rid of everything that does not please God before coming before Him in worship. Jacob recognized that the Lord, the true God, helped him to escape his anguish and in gratitude built an altar to Him.

A grateful heart of God delights in praise and blesses God for all his wonders. Real praise is spontaneous and springs from the depths of a soul that has been redeemed from sin. The Word of God exhorts us to praise God, regardless of what we may be going through. If we could weigh both the good and the bad things in our lives, I am totally convinced that the good things would far outweigh the bad. Our minds, however, tend to focus on the bad while blurring the good.

God knew that his people needed a place to settle, to develop and grow. This is why he commanded them to conquer and occupy the land of Canaan (Num 13:25). God instructed Moses to send 12 spies into the land. What great disappointment Moses experienced when ten of the spies brought him a negative report. They focused on the negative things they were able to see with their human eyes, namely the giant inhabitants of the land. But God always has a remnant—in this case, Joshua and Caleb, two courageous men who had also gone to Canaan along with the ten spies. Unlike the 12, Joshua and Caleb brought back a positive report of hope. They were firmly convinced that God would give them victory and that they would defeat the giants (Num. 13:30): "And Caleb stilled the people before Moses, and said, Let us go up at once, and possess it; for we are well able to overcome it." These two men had their eyes on the promises of God. They did not look at the obstacles or the difficulties they could face because they claimed God's promise to Abraham in Genesis 12:7: "And the LORD appeared unto Abram, and said, Unto thy seed will I give this land: and there build he an altar unto the LORD, who appeared unto him."

Despite their optimism, there was a great resistance as the rest of the people, together with the other ten spies, did not agree with them. They even tried to stone them (Numbers 14:10). The negative report about the giants and fortresses managed to intimidate the people very quickly. One would think that obstacles such as these could have intimidated anyone except the people of Israel because they served a

Where do you start?

God who had shown his power in myriad occasions. They had been eyewitnesses to the parting of the Red Sea. They had been fed for years with manna from heaven. They wore the same clothes and sandals day in and day out, yet had no need to replace them. As if that were not enough, they were accompanied by the very presence of God in the form of a pillar of clouds by day and at night as a pillar of fire. The more God blessed them, the more they complained.

Psalms 100:4 says, "Enter his gates with thanksgiving and his courts with praise." There are many ways that you can praise God, here are some of them:

- **With Songs: Psalms 9:11** "Sing praises to the LORD, which dwelleth in Zion: declare among the people his doings"
- **With musical instruments: Psalm 150:3-5** "Praise him with the sound of the trumpet: praise him with the psaltery and harp. Praise him with the timbrel and dance: praise him with stringed instruments and organs. Praise him upon the loud cymbals: praise him upon the high sounding cymbals."
- **With dance: 2 Samuel 6:21** "And David said unto Michal, It was before the LORD, which chose me before thy father, and before all his house, to appoint me ruler over the people of the LORD, over Israel: therefore will I play before the LORD."
- **With our witness: Psalms 67:3** "Let the people praise thee, O God; let all the people praise thee."

In the book of Acts chapter 16 verse 11 onwards, Paul and Silas met a girl who had a spirit of divination that made her master a great deal of money. Paul and Silas noticed that this spirit was not of God. Filled with the authority and power of God, he rebuked the spirit that tormented her, and she was instantly free. Later, the girl's masters became angry and sought to have them imprisoned. After being beaten, as it was ordered by the judge, they threw them into prison and placed them under maximum security. The jailer placed them in the dungeon. The shackles on their feet were fastened to the jail wall. The human mind cannot comprehend the events in verse 25. The men were filled with the power of God and at midnight, Paul and Silas were praying and singing hymns to God while the other prisoners listened. A sudden earthquake shook the foundations of the prison, and the doors flew open. The chains fell off their body and all the prisoners were set free. I can imagine the jailer's amazement.

This is the key to your victory. No matter what the enemy has done to keep you in bondage, even in the midst of your spiritual imprisonment, start to praise God. If you feel weak, praise him softly. 1 Corinthians 1:25 says, "For the weakness of God is stronger than the man." 2 Corinthians 12:10 says, "Because when I am weak, then I am strong." Hebrews 13:15 says: "So, always offer to God by means of the sacrifice of praise, that is to say, the fruit of lips that confess his name." If you feel tired, praise him. Isaiah 40:29 says, "He gives strength to the weary and increases the power of he that has none." If you are feeling sleepy, praise him. Psalm 57:8

says: "Awake, my soul; awake, psaltery and harp." If you feel faint, continue praising him. Jonah 2:7 says: "When my soul was fainting in me, I remembered the Lord, and my prayer came to you in your holy temple." Don't miss the opportunity to praise him and to thank him for all his blessings Even if the situation worsens, remember that it is darkest just before dawn. Praise and worship moves the rafters of heaven. 1 Chronicles 16:29 says, "Give unto the LORD the glory due unto his name: bring an offering, and come before him: worship the LORD in the beauty of holiness." Psalms 95:6 says: "O come, let us worship and bow down: let us kneel before the LORD our maker." John 4:24 says, "God is a Spirit: and they that worship him must worship him in spirit and in truth." If you look closely, these scriptures commanded us to worship God—that is why we were created. Oh beloved reader, don't forget the importance and the power of praise. Be encouraged by the power of God and take back that which was taken away from you. Take possession of God's promises; take ownership of all of them. Begin to take firm steps, steps of faith in the Lord. Declare things that are not as if they were. Ask God and consider it done, by faith. Deposit your burdens upon him and continue to praise him. Soar into your spiritual conquest. God has many blessings for your life that were blocked by anguish. Begin to receive those blessings. Proverbs 10:22 says, "The blessing of the LORD, it maketh rich, and he addeth no sorrow with it." Note that the Word of God says in 2Corinthians 10:4, "For the weapons of our warfare are not carnal, but mighty through God to the pulling down of strong holds," for destruction of fortresses. Ephesians 6:11-12 tells us: "Put on the whole armour of God, that ye may be able to stand against the wiles of the devil. For we wrestle not against flesh and blood, but against principalities, against powers, against the rulers of the darkness of this world, against spiritual wickedness in high places." Three disciplines are necessary in order to emerge victorious in this fight: prayer, fasting, and reading the Word of God. This formula—accompanied by adoration, praise, and a spotless testimony, will result in your victorious life in Christ Jesus. 1 Kings 8:56 says: "Blessed be the LORD that hath given rest unto his people Israel, according to all that he promised: there hath not failed one word of all his good promise, which he promised by the hand of Moses his servant."

All of us would like to live happy lives regardless of what we are facing. Gratitude is essential to happiness. When you're grateful, you will see things in a totally different way. There are seven steps to maintain an attitude of gratitude:

1. Remember how fortunate and blessed you are. Many times, we believe we need many things, when in reality, they are not absolutely necessary. You must realize how rich you are. Count your blessings and all the good things you have. This is what actually enriches us. The valuable things in life do not cost anything.

Where do you start?

2. Consider the health and life that God has granted you. Some people do not have the opportunity to live beyond 20-35 years. You can move freely and do things without difficulty. You have the freedom to make decisions by yourself, without fear of coercion.
3. Think about how good it is to live in peace. Many people live in countries that are currently at war. They live in fear of dying every day.
4. Consider all the good things that are happening around you. The mere fact that you have someone whom you consider a friend is a blessing.
5. Begin to identify your blessings. If possible, write them in a notebook. This will help you keep them in mind every day.
6. Focus on giving and not so much on receiving. The Bible says that it is better to give than to receive. Many people focus on receiving and on the things they lack that it becomes difficult for them to be grateful.
7. Decide to be a grateful person. Live one day at a time. Mention God's blessings day after day. From the moment you open your eyes in the morning, give thanks to God for one more day of life that He gives you. Do not allow the negative things in your daily life take away your attitude of gratitude.

At present there are many people in prisons that are freer than many who walk freely in the streets. As absurd as it may seem,

DELIVER ME FROM MY ANGUISH, LORD!

in our streets there are thousands and thousands of people who are oppressed, most of them by a spirit of anguish. I have known people who have gone to jail and there they have had the opportunity to know Christ and today they preach the word in prison, feeling totally free because they have understood that God allowed them to get to that place with a purpose. I have heard testimonies of people who have spent many years in prison and did not want to leave because they did not know how to act in the free world. There are many people who are so bound by anguish that they have developed a co-dependency on it and do not want to be free because they would not know how to act outside their spiritual prison. They do not understand God's plan for their lives; therefore, they do not seek freedom, preferring to remain in anguish and oppression.

Let us remember that when the Apostle Paul wrote the book of Ephesians, he was a prisoner (Ephesians 6:20): "For which I am an ambassador in bonds: that therein I may speak boldly, as I ought to speak." However, chains were not reason enough for him to be sad, nor did they take away his desire to worship God. He neither cried nor lamented his situation. He took advantage of those moments to write everything the Holy Spirit told him to write. He felt a burden to speak boldly about what God had done in his life. When we break free from the things that displease God—sin, we can be truly free. Romans 8:21 says: "Because the creature itself also shall be delivered from the bondage of corruption into the glorious liberty of the children of God." We can feel liberty in Christ when we make Him

Master and Lord of our lives. 2 Corinthians 3:17 puts it this way: "Now the Lord is that Spirit: and where the Spirit of the Lord is, there is liberty." Looking at the inverse of that statement, we could say that where the Spirit of God is not present, there is no freedom or liberty. Therefore, we can conclude that we need the Spirit of God in our lives to be free indeed. Galatians 5:1 says, "Stand fast therefore in the liberty wherewith Christ hath made us free, and be not entangled again with the yoke of bondage."

The Spirit of Anguish Will Mold Our Character

Pay close attention to this truth: The character of an adult, together with his personality, is the product of what he has enjoyed, what he has suffered, and how he has reacted in the face of adversity during his formative years. The way you react to adversity reveals your true character. If you tend to get desperate and lose your peace easily when you face adversity, then you should seek to mold your character.

I have come across many people whose world has changed because of anguish. Instead of getting closer to God, they have opted to stay away from him. They feel that God has moved away from them. Jeremiah felt it in Lamentations 1:16: "For these things I weep; mine eye, mine eye runneth down with water, because the comforter that should relieve my soul is far from me: my children are desolate, because the enemy prevailed." Jesus promised his disciples that he would send the Comforter, which would guide them into all truth and justice. The Comforter, the Holy Spirit, came to give us power (Acts 1:8): "But ye shall receive power, after that the Holy Ghost is come upon you: and ye shall be witnesses unto me both in Jerusalem, and in all Judaea, and in Samaria, and unto the uttermost part of the earth." This power transforms men. The Peter who denied Jesus at the time of Jesus' arrest is not the same Peter who was filled with the Holy Spirit. There was a big difference in his character. Even if we had been there, we probably would not believe it to be the same person. The disciples could have been crying and lamenting the fact that their teacher was gone. They could have reminisced about all the times spent with the Master and wishing that He was still among them. Instead, there was work to be done, and they could not allow crying and anguish to take over their lives. They were to obey the words of the Master and go to the upper room to await the promise.

Other people who are in the midst of anguish look for another source of comfort, rather than turning to God. Jeremiah 2:13 says: "For my people have committed two evils; they have forsaken me the fountain of living waters, and hewed them out cisterns, broken cisterns, that can hold no water." Many people promise many things, including freedom and comfort, to those who feel distressed. Some counseling programs, yoga, transcendental meditation, and other religious practices deceive many people. Today, palm readers are on every corner. Others have formed religions that promise "no more suffering." The Apostle Peter in his second epistle, chapter 2 verse 19, explains: "While they promise them liberty, they themselves are the servants of corruption: for of whom a man is overcome, of the same is he brought in bondage."

Jesus clearly said it in His word: "I am the way, the truth and the life and no one comes to the Father, if it is not by me." Then in John 8:32: "And ye shall know the truth, and the truth shall make you free." And on verse 36: "If the Son therefore shall make you free, ye shall be free indeed." In a nutshell, we know that only through Jesus can we be set free from a spirit of anguish.

I want to invite you to consider this a good time to accept Jesus Christ as your Lord and Savior, if you have not already had a personal experience with Him. He is the answer to all your problems. You must simply agree to accept this truth: Christ, the Son of God, became man. He taught and preached and performed miracles to help us. He died for our sins and rose from the dead on the third day. He ascended into heaven and now offers salvation to all who believe in Him and one day will return for his church (his people). Romans 10:9-11 says, "That if thou shalt confess with thy mouth the Lord Jesus, and shalt believe in thine heart that God hath raised him from the dead, thou shalt be saved. For with the heart man believeth unto righteousness; and with the mouth confession is made unto salvation. For the scripture saith, whosoever believeth on him shall not be ashamed."

It is possible that your world has been disrupted overnight. Maybe you used to be a happy person, but pain and desperation came to your door and you are no longer that person. This can happen to anyone. The Bible says that many are the afflictions of the just, but God assures us that he will deliver us from them all. It is very easy to

The Spirit of Anguish Will Mold Our Character

tell someone to change their attitude when one has experienced their situation, but we must also recognize that we have a God of power. Pain and scars in a person's heart can hurt and be very intense. The cry of anguish can literally hurt the heart and feel like it will never end. But with God, nothing is impossible. God can heal your broken heart and heal your wounds. Our human mind can never fully comprehend God's love toward us. When Christ died on the cross of Calvary, he took with him all our diseases and our ailments. In Christ, there is hope for a new beginning. All is not lost; we're still alive, and God has not yet finished with you. We know this with all certainty because Philippians 1:6 says: "Being confident of this very thing, that he which hath begun a good work in you will perform it until the day of Jesus Christ." We cannot allow others to lead us to believe otherwise. You are a child of God called to live in victory. Deuteronomy 28:13 says: "And the LORD shall make thee the head, and not the tail; and thou shalt be above only, and thou shalt not be beneath; if that thou hearken unto the commandments of the LORD thy God, which I command thee this day, to observe and to do them." The Apostle Peter in his first epistle, chapter 2 verses 9-10 said: "But ye are a chosen generation, a royal priesthood, an holy nation, a peculiar people; that ye should shew forth the praises of him who hath called you out of darkness into his marvellous light; Which in time past were not a people, but are now the people of God: which had not obtained mercy, but now have obtained mercy." God chose you and me for a very clear purpose: To announce his wonders to the entire world. An anguished heart cannot proclaim the wonders of God. Later in the same chapter, in verses 21-22, Peter said: "For even hereunto were ye called: because Christ also suffered for us, leaving us an example, that ye should follow his steps: Who did no sin, neither was guile found in his mouth."

Job said something that stirs within me: "Though he may slay me, I will wait in him." Job had such great faith. He recognized the power of God so much so that he dared to express: "I know that my Redeemer lives, and even of the same dust he will lift me up." You and I as children of God have a divine deliverer. In 2 Corinthians 1:10, the Apostle reminds us: "Who delivered us from so great a death, and doth deliver: in whom we trust that he will yet deliver us." Daniel 6:27 declares: "He delivereth and rescueth, and he worketh signs and wonders in heaven and in earth, who hath delivered Daniel from the power of the lions." In Isaiah 46:4, God promise His people: "And even to your old age I am he; and even to hoar hairs will I carry you: I have made, and I will bear; even I will carry, and will deliver you." Isaiah 59:19 says: "So shall they fear the name of the LORD from the west, and his glory from the rising of the sun. When the enemy shall come in like a flood, the Spirit of the LORD shall lift up a standard against him."

A radical change occurs in a person who has been set free from a spirit of anguish. This change is very noticeable and it begins from the inside out. The person begins to exhibit the fruits of the spirit: love, joy, peace, patience, kindness, goodness, faith, meekness and

The Spirit of Anguish Will Mold Our Character

temperance. He also begins to make wise decisions, seeking to straighten that which is crooked in their life. They start showing interest in the Word of God and begin looking for a closer relationship with the Lord Jesus Christ. They also seem to be more concerned in making others happy and start thinking less about themselves. We might say that they go through a total transformation. They also begin to get rid of the things that do not please God and were holding them back from fellowship with Him. The person also learns to trust that God has control of everything that happens in their life. God begins to reveal things to the person that they could not see or understand when they were blinded by anguish. The person has a higher level of spiritual maturity as they fellowship with God. Their entire life is now different.

The years that we live on earth are very short compared to eternal life. God wants us to enjoy life in every sense of the word. He doesn't want us to be in anguish and has promised to lift our burdens from our shoulders. Jesus said: "I came that you may have life and life more abundantly." Won't you decide to be happy today and enjoy that abundant life that He is offering you? The following points will help you through the process.

- Regardless of what you're going through, there is someone else who is going through the same thing or even through something worse. 1 Peter 4: **12.** "Beloved, think it not strange concerning the fiery trial which is to try you, as though some strange thing happened unto you: **13.** But rejoice, inasmuch as ye are partakers of Christ's sufferings; that, when his glory shall be revealed, ye may be glad also with exceeding joy."

- Forget about yourself and worry more about others. Mathew 10:42: "And whosoever shall give to drink unto one of these little ones a cup of cold water only in the name of a disciple, verily I say unto you, he shall in no wise lose his reward." Isaiah 58:7 says, "Is it not to deal thy bread to the hungry, and that thou bring the poor that are cast out to thy house? When thou seest the naked, that thou cover him; and that thou hide not thyself from thine own flesh?"

- It's possible that as of today, your past has been playing a very important role in your present. Decide that even though you're not where you'd like to be, nor do you have what you wish you had, you're going to move forward and not allow your present circumstances dictate your future. Philippians 1:6 says, "Being confident of this very thing, that he which hath begun a good work in you will perform it until the day of Jesus Christ." Also, Philippians 3: **13.** Brethren, I count not myself to have apprehended: but this one thing I do, forgetting those things which are behind, and reaching forth unto those things which are before, **14.** I press toward the mark for the prize of the high calling of God in Christ Jesus."

- Slow down, you may be going too fast through line. Life is journey that is only walked once. Learn to enjoy the small things in life. Don't walk too fast, you may be missing out a lot, God is a god of details. Stop to look at the greatness of God around you. Psalms 31:7 says, "I will be glad and rejoice in thy mercy: for thou hast considered my trouble; thou hast known my soul in adversities." " **Psalms 71:17:** O God, thou hast taught me from my youth: and hitherto have I declared thy wondrous works.

- Don't surround yourself with losers. Choose people who are optimistic and refuse to be influenced by negative comments. Pick your acquaintances carefully, after all they will have an impact on your decisions and their outcome. Ecclesiastes 7:21-22 says, "Also take no heed unto all words that are spoken; lest thou hear thy servant curse thee: For oftentimes also thine own heart knoweth that thou thyself likewise hast cursed others."
- Organize your thoughts and ideas as well as everything that happens to you in one of these three ways:
  - Resolve them: Do what is necessary to make them a reality.
  - Capitalize on them and allow them to lead you to the next level.
  - Abandon and release them by giving them over to God.

The Apostle Paul learned to be content no matter what the situation.1 Thessalonians 1:6 said, "And ye became followers of us, and of the Lord, having received the word in much affliction, with joy of the Holy Ghost."

Many people are satisfied surviving day after day, but they are merely existing because have not learned to enjoy their life to the fullest. When they come to realize this, they are usually old and have not known the joys of life. Psalm 90:9 says that we spend our years as a tale that is told. I am not talking about having a smile on your face all the time, nor having something that entertains you 24 hours a day. This is about having contentment, the indescribable joy of God. Each circumstance in our life is an opportunity to move forward. When we recall the past, it should serve as a lesson for spiritual growth. When others see the peace of God on your face, they are going to want what you have. Your happiness will become contagious. I challenge to you to seek freedom from the spirit of anguish, putting in practice the advice that I have given you in this book and trying to live every day with joy. You may probably think that it sounds too easy to be true, because you still have much fear, but 2 Timothy 1:7 reads: "For God hath not given us the spirit of fear; but of power, and of love, and of a sound mind."

Studies have demonstrated that only two percent of people stop to self-evaluate themselves. Many people do not reach their goals and objectives in life because they have not stopped to identify their "passion." A person focused on their "passion" is not likely to be tormented by a spirit of anguish. Below, I have detailed four basic steps that will help you to focus on developing your passion or any other area of your life that you wish you pursue. You can apply these steps to your personal, as well as your spiritual, life.

The Spirit of Anguish Will Mold Our Character

<u>First Step</u>: Begin a deep process of studying your present situation this will help you Identify your real passion. You may do this by asking yourself the following questions:

- Where I am at this moment of my life?
- What things are important to me?
- What things do I enjoy doing?
- What motivates me?
- What are my strong areas and my weaknesses?

<u>Second Step</u>: Lead your passion. Once you have discovered what your passion is or may be, continue the preparation process to reach your goal.

- How can my present experience help me in my passion?
- How I can find opportunities to help me reach my goal?
- What steps must I follow?

<u>Third Step</u>: Don't lose focus of your passion

- How far do I want to go? (Local, International etc.
- How will this affect my family and my present lifestyle?
- Which opportunity or decision will best benefit those around me?

<u>Fourth Step</u>: Take action by walking toward your passion

- Make sure you know: What is the next step toward my passion?
- Is my plan realistic and attainable?
- Am I progressing on the path toward my goal?

By using these basic steps you will remain focused, you will have a plan and you will have a list of skills and behaviors required to reach your passion.

You can use your experiences to develop and grow your passion. Your good and your bad experiences can be used as a stepping stool to reach your goal. Remember: The more you know about your abilities, talents and skills, the more opportunities you will have to develop your passion. Most of all, be persistent and never give up. Ephesians 5: "14. Wherefore he saith, Awake thou that sleepest, and arise from the dead, and Christ shall give thee light. 15. See then that ye walk circumspectly, not as fools, but as wise, 16. Redeeming the time, because the days are evil. 17. Wherefore be ye not unwise, but understanding what the will of the Lord is."

God Loved Us First

I want to close this book with a final word that permeates everything I have said throughout each of these pages. It's about the love of God. Many people have moved away from God because they have been hurt by someone, and they think that God does not love them anymore. This has caused them much anguish, and they do not know how to find their way back to God. We were taught all of our lives that we must love God, but many missed the opportunity to mention that this is because he loved us first. 1 John 4:10-11 says: "Herein is love, not that we loved God, but that he loved us, and sent his Son to be the propitiation for our sins. Beloved, if God so loved us, we ought also to love one another."

You see, the Bible says that we were all destined to eternal torment; there was no hope of salvation. Therefore, we could not aspire to eternity in heaven. Romans 3:23 "For all have sinned and come short of the glory of God." But God In his great mercy has opened the door to salvation to all those who accept the sacrifice of his son Jesus Christ in the cross of Calvary.

When God looks at us, He does not see us as men see us. He looks at us through the sacrifice of his begotten son Jesus on Calvary's cross. It is through this sacrifice that we can be sure that once we reach His presence, He will receive us with open arms and make us part of the family of God. 1 John 3:1 says, "Behold, what manner of love the Father hath bestowed upon us, that we should be called the sons of God: therefore the world knoweth us not, because it knew him not." 1 John 4, verses 17 to 19 say, "Herein is our love made perfect, that we may have boldness in the Day of Judgment: because as he is, so are we in this world. There is no fear in love; but perfect love casteth out fear: because fear hath torment. He that feareth is not made perfect in love. We love him, because he first loved us."

This is a matter of attitude. Which attitude will you adopt? If you adopt a positive attitude in life, God will see to it that all things work together for good for you. Remember that greater is He that is in you, than he that is in the world (1John 4:4). No matter what you may be going through, no matter how bad your past may have been, no matter if you think that no one loves you, no matter if you think everything has been lost, God is telling you today: Revelation 3:20 "Behold, I stand at the door, and knock: if any man hear my voice, and open the door, I will come in to him, and will sup with him, and he with me."

If this book has been a blessing to your life, I would love to hear from your. Please write us at Paredes_de_Amor@yahoo.com. May God Bless your life richly!

Bibliography

Holy Bible King James Version -1960 edition.

Personal consultation with Rosita Sierra, mental health professional, Tampa, Florida, USA.

Complete works of Sigmund Freud. Standard Edition. Sorting of James Strachey. Volume XVI. Conferences introduction to psychoanalysis. part III, general doctrine of the neurosis (1917 [16-17]). Lecture 25, anguish.

Complete works of Sigmund Freud. Standard Edition. Sorting of James Strachey. Volume XX. Inhibitions, symptoms and anxiety (1926 [1925])

Complete works of Sigmund Freud. Standard Edition. Sorting of James Strachey. Volume XXII. New conferences introduction to Psicoanalysis (1933 [1932]). Conference 32, anguish and drives of life.

Other links of information online motivational links.

Wiktionary has an entry on anguish

TuOtroyo medico.com

Reading and commentary of the seminar "Anguish" de J. Lacan

Information on problems of Mental health of "http://es.wikipedia.org/wiki/Anguish"

CPSIA information can be obtained at www.ICGtesting.com
Printed in the USA
LVOW07s1439220816

501361LV00001B/353/P